DBMM Army Lists

Book 1: The Chariot Period
3000 BC to 500 BC

Revised Edition

by Phil Barker

For use with the Be Bellis Magistrorum Militum wargame rules.

A Wargames Research Group Limited Publication   **2016**

First edition published in 2009 by Partizan Press,

Revised edition published in 2016 by
Wargames Research Group Ltd
208 Mill Road,
Cambridge CB1 3NF.

www.wargamesresearchgroup.net

ISBN 978-0-244-52049-6

Front cover notes
The front cover shows Rameses II in his chariot in battle against the Hittites.He is wearing a crown with a cobra, a blue and gold striped robe, and aiming a bow and arrow at his enemies who are shown falling beneath his horses. The image is taken from Histoire de l'Art Egyptien by Emile Prisse d'Avennes and P. Marchandon de la Faye which depicts ancient Egyptian paintings and carvings and was originally published in Paris 1878-9.

Contents

INTRODUCTION

These lists are intended for use with the "De Bellis Magistrorum Militum" wargames rules, more familiarly known as "DBMM". While mainly intended for competition games, they also provide a general guide to armies' troop classification and proportions for use in conjunction with more detailed sources, such as the WRG army handbooks. Each list is designed to produce 300 AP to 500 AP armies that closely simulate their real life prototype, while still allowing sufficient flexibility to cover historical variations during the period and legitimate differences of opinion or personal preference. Most include about 200 AP of compulsory troops and allow greater freedom of choice for the remainder, this choice diminishing as the size of the army increases. AP are set to give armies approximately equal combat value over the full range of likely battlefield conditions and opponents. This is not an exact science!

Most lists correspond to the previous DBM lists compiled by myself and Richard Bodley Scott, but have been extensively modified; both to provide the extra information required by DBMM, and in the light further very high quality research by many people, including the TNE internet group and members of DBMMlist@yahoogroups.com. The period covered has been extended to include the first part of the Great Italian and early Tudor wars when armies were still medieval in type. Although these lists have been very much a collective project and consensus has always been sought, this has not always been possible, and I alone am responsible for the final decisions. Where there is disagreement about the more obscure troop types or only minor doubt, I have sometimes chosen to specify only the interpretation I think most likely. This has been done not through hubris, but for the sake of simplicity, and to reduce the scope for tailoring of armies by over-competitive players. Where a decision has been finely balanced, I have chosen the interpretation producing the most realistic effect against the army's historical opponents.

The first part of each list comprises troops available throughout the historical time period covered. Some armies then have additional sub-lists of troops available only to particular historical generals, or only in specific geographical regions, or during only part of the period. An army including troops only available to a particular general cannot include troops available only to a different general. An army including troops only available in a particular geographical area cannot include troops available only in a different geographical area. An army including troops available only in a particular historical period cannot include troops available only during an incompatible historical period. An army must have a commander-in-chief (C-in-C) and at least one other general. No army can have more than four generals.

Where troop types are separated by "or", any mixture of them can be used, unless they are preceded by "all"; in which case only one of the types can be used. When a ratio such as "up to ½" is used, this is ½ those used, not ½ the maximum permitted.

ALLIES

To qualify as an ally, a nation must have arrived or attempted to arrive in aid at a historical battle. In most cases foreign allied contingents are specified by reference to their own list. Each such allied contingent must include a single general, who (unless exceptional reliability causes them to be specified in the employing army's list as sub-generals) are ally-generals. Their type can be that of the allied contingent's list's specified C-in-C or sub-general. Unless otherwise specified in a particular list, the allied contingent can otherwise include only compulsory troop types, and must have at least a quarter of the specified minimum number of elements of each such type. It cannot include more than a third of the specified maximum number of each such type, or 1 element, whichever is greater. In some cases the maximum total number of elements that can be included in the allied contingent, including the general but not baggage elements, is specified. An allied command of less than 10 troop elements cannot have more than 1 baggage element.

Unless otherwise specified by either of the 2 lists, allied troops cannot be used outside their own army's date range, and can use only those options specified in their own list for the assisted army's date, and any minima or maxima for upgrades are modified as above. The full allowance of troops listed in the form "0-1 per X" can be included for each "X" element included. An allied contingent cannot include allies of its own. Unless otherwise specified, only one foreign allied contingent of each nationality can be included.

Where foreign allies do not have a suitable list of their own, their contingent is specified as a sub-list within a nation's main list. In this case the minimum and maximum number of elements of each troop type will be as specified in that sub-list. Where ally generals are specified in a nation's main list, such generals are of the same or a closely related nationality. Unlike foreign irregular ally generals, they will never change sides except in a civil war (between armies of the same list and nationality), and may then do so whether regular or irregular. Each such general's command must, unless stated otherwise, include at least a quarter of the minimum number of each compulsory troop type. It can also include non-compulsory types. All elements count towards the total number of each type specified in the list.

NAVAL

Naval elements are included only if they played a significant part in a mainly land battle. Each replaces a land element of the list, of the type or types that follow it within brackets. For example, a Greek trieres/trireme element Reg Gal (F) @ 4AP [Sp or Ps], replaces one of the compulsory or optional Sp or Ps elements of the army list, and can disembark that element. The AP quoted is for the trieres only. The embarked element must still be paid for. Naval elements with no landing troops specified cannot provide landing parties. AP spent on naval elements are wasted if they have no access on to the table. Their landing troops and baggage can still be deployed, being assumed to have disembarked and joined the army prior to the battle. Landing troops specified as equal to the number of available vessels (such as marines, sailors or oarsmen) can be used only if the vessels are paid for.

FORTIFICATIONS

Any army with BUA listed among its permitted terrain types can have sufficient permanent fortifications (PF) or temporary fortifications (TF) to enclose the on-table part of a BUA if it is the defender. PF must be part of a BUAf. No other PF are permitted. TF not enclosing a BUA can only be used if specified by the army's list. Those specified as defending camps or baggage must have each end touching their side's rear battlefield edge or a water feature or marsh and contain baggage. Points spent on fortifications other than those specified by the army's list are wasted if the terrain includes no suitable BUA, or the army is the invader.

CLIMATE, AGGRESSION AND TERRAIN

The first line of each list's heading specifies the army's home climate, its aggression factor, and codes for the types of terrain that can be chosen if it is the defender. Types in **underlined bold** are compulsory. Where types are separated by "or", only one of these types can be chosen. If they are separated by "and", both or neither must be used. Even if not listed, a single patch of coastal sand dunes or marsh can always be used if successfully positioned in contact with a sea, or a single patch of marsh if successfully positioned in contact with a river. Terrain types are:

S	Sea.	FS	Sea that may freeze in Winter.		
WW	Waterway.	L	Lake.	Rv	River.
DH	Difficult steep hill.	CH	Craggy steep hill.	WH	Wooded hill.
RH	Rocky gentle low hill.	SH	Scrubby gentle low hill.	GH	Bare gentle low hill.
BUA	Built-up area.	BUAf	BUA if optionally allowed PF.	FW	Frontier wall.
Rd	Unpaved roads or frequently used tracks.			PRd	Paved road.
F	Large open fields.	E	Small enclosed fields.	B	Boundary hedge or wall.
O	Orchard or olive grove.	Oa	Desert oasis.	V	Vineyards.
Wd	Wood.	M	Marsh.	D	Sand dunes.
BF	Boggy flat ground.	SF	Scrub-covered flat ground.	RF	Rocky flat ground.
G	Sunken gully.				

Hills are gentle if their slope gives a significant combat advantage but does not slow men or animals unless there is significant surface cover. Difficult hills have slopes that significantly slow movement, whatever their surface cover. Wooded hills can be steep or gentle. Slopes that do not give a significant advantage or slow movement are treated as flat ground and not represented as hills.

The home terrain of an empire is assumed to be that of its heartland or capital, the centre of its power. The home terrain of a migration is that of the last region occupied before entering on the stage of world history. That of rebellious mercenaries is their previous area of operations. Terrain types are restricted to those that are typical of the area. Rarer types are allowed only if they significantly influenced a historical battle or were on a historically used invasion route. An oasis differs from an orchard in being of palm trees with often an under-crop or pool and usually being larger.

ARMIES INCLUDED IN BOOK 1

1. Early Sumerian. 3000 BC - 2334 BC and c. 2250 BC
2. Early Egyptian. 3000 BC - 1541 BC
3. Nubian. 3000 BC - 1480 BC
4. Zagros and Anatolian Highlanders. 3000 BC - 950 BC
5. Early Susiana and Elam. 3000 BC - 800 BC
6. Early Bedouin. 3000 BC - 312 BC
7. Early Libyan. 3000 BC - 70 AD
8. Makkan, Dilmun, Saba, Ma'in and Qataban. 2800 BC - 312 BC
9. Early Syrian. 2700 BC - 2200 BC
10. Melukhkhan or Pre-Vedic Indian. 2700 BC - 1500 BC
11. Akkadian, Third Dynasty of Ur. 2334 BC - 2004 BC
12. Sumerian Successor States. 2028 BC - 1460 BC
13. Hsia and Shang Chinese. 2000 BC - 1017 BC
14. Early Northern Barbarians. 2000 BC - 315 BC
15. Later Amorite. 1894 BC - 1595 BC
16. Hittite Old and Middle Kingdom. 1680 BC - 1380 BC
17. Hyksos. 1645 BC - 1537 BC
18. Minoan and Early Mycenaean. 1600 BC - 1250 BC
19. Mitanni. 1595 BC - 1274 BC
20. Syro-Canaanite and Ugaritic. 1595 BC - 1100 BC
21. Kassite and Later Babylonian. 1595 BC - 747 BC
22. New Kingdom Egyptian. 1543 BC - 1069 BC
23. Vedic Indian. 1500 BC - 512 BC
24. Hittite Empire. 1380 BC - 1170 BC
25. Middle and Early Neo-Assyrian. 1365 BC - 745 BC
26. Later Mycenaean and Trojan War. 1250 BC - 1190 BC
27. Early Hebrew. 1250 BC - 1000 BC
28. Sea Peoples. 1208 BC - 1176 BC
29. Philistine. 1166 BC - 600 BC
30. Dark Age and Geometric Greek. 1160 BC - 650 BC
31. Neo-Hittite and Later Aramaean. 1100 BC -710 BC
32. Western Chou and Spring and Autumn Chinese. 1100 BC - 480 BC
33. Villanovan Italian. 1000 BC -650 AD
34. Later Hebrew. 1000 BC - 650 BC
35. Cypriot and Phoenician. 1000 BC - 332 BC
36. Italian Hill Tribes. 1000 BC - 124 BC
37. Mannaian, and other Taurus and Zagros states. 950 BC - 610 BC
38. Libyan Egyptian. 946 BC - 712 BC
39. Urartian. 880 BC - 585 BC
40. Phrygian. 850 BC - 676 BC
41. Medes, Zikirtu, Andia or Parsua. 835 BC - 550 BC
42. Neo-Elamite. 800 BC - 639 BC
43. Kimmerian, Skythian or Early Hu. 750 BC- 50 AD
44. Neo-Babylonian. 746 BC - 482 BC
45. Neo-Assyrian Empire. 745 BC - 681 BC
46. Kushite Egyptian. 745 BC - 593 BC
47. Illyrian. 700 BC - 10 AD
48. Thracian. 700 BC - 46 AD
49. Early Vietnamese. 700 BC - 938 AD
50. Lydian. 687 BC - 540 BC
51. Later Sargonid Assyrian. 680 BC - 609 BC
52. Early Hoplite Greek. 669 BC - 449 BC
53. Saitic Egyptian. 664 BC - 335 BC
54. Early Macedonian. 650 BC - 355 BC
55. Latin, Early Roman, Early Etruscan and Umbrian Italian. 650 BC to 290 BC
56. Kyrenean Greek. 630 BC - 74 BC
57. Etruscan League. 600 BC - 280 BC
58. Meroitic Kushite. 592 BC - 350 AD
59. Tullian Roman. 578 BC - 400 BC
60. Early Achaemenid Persian. 550 BC - 420 BC
61. Early Carthaginian. 550 BC - 275 BC
62. Lykian. 546 BC - 300 BC
63. Paionian. 512 BC -284 BC
64. Early Japanese. 500 BC -500 AD

NATURAL ENEMIES

The armies that are most plausible historical enemies are listed by book and army number after the permitted home terrain

DATE RANGES

An army entered for a competition or used in a friendly game (and any ally contingents) must be specified as of a single specific year and include only troops available in that year.

The terms "before", "after", "from", "between" and "from/to" have the following meanings:

- Before 1000 BC means the year 1000 BC and later years are excluded.
- After 1000 BC means the year 1000 BC and earlier years are excluded.
- From 1000 BC means the year 1000 BC and later years are included.
- Between 2000 BC and 1000 BC or from 2000 BC to 1000 BC both mean the years 2000 BC and 1000 BC and all years between are included.

LANGUAGE

Place names are those in English language histories and may differ from those in a modern atlas. Personal and technical names are those used by the people the list covers or their enemies, except for personal names familiar in their anglicised form such as Philip, Alexander and Pompey. Chinese names are transliterated using the old Wade-Giles system, which (unlike the modern Pinyin system favoured by the Chinese government) enables an English speaker to approximate Chinese pronunciation (DBMMlist@yahoogroups.com has an equivalence table for modernists). Arabic names are transliterated by the usual modern system, but older systems differ in spelling not pronunciation - for example "Khalif" and "Caliph" are obviously the same word.

TROOP TYPE ABBREVIATIONS

Abbreviations used in these lists for troop types and artificial features are: El = Elephants. Exp = Expendables. Kn = Knights. Cv = Cavalry. LH = Light Horse. Cm = Camelry. Sp = Spears. Pk = Pikes. Bd = Blades. Wb = Warband. Ax = Auxilia. Bw = Bows. Sh = Shot. Ps = Psiloi. Art = Artillery. WWg = War Wagons. Hd = Hordes. Gal = Galleys. Shp = Ships. Bts = Boats. Bge = Baggage. Mtd = Mounted Infantry, PF = permanent fortifications, TF = temporary fortifications, FO = fixed obstacle, HO = FO used as a Hidden Obstacle stratagem, PO = portable obstacle.

SOURCES OF FURTHER INFORMATION ON THE ARMIES INCLUDED IN BOOK 1

Further information on the organisation, equipment, tactics and appearance of the majority of the armies in these army list books can be found in the WRG series of army books. Particularly relevant to Book 1 is:

Armies of the Ancient Near East 3,000 BC to 539 BC by Nigel Stillman and Nigel Tallis.

Other useful books include:
The Achaemenid Persian Army by Duncan Head - Montvert - ISBN 1 874101 00 0
Warfare in the Ancient Near East to 1600 BC by William J. Hamblin - Routledge - ISBN 0 415 25589 9
Battles of the Bible by Chaim Herzog and Mordechai Gichon - Random House - ISBN 394 50131 4
The Art of Warfare in Biblical Lands by Yigael Yadin - Weidenfeld & Nicolson 1963

The New Penguin Atlas of Ancient History by Colin McEvedy and David Woodroffe is especially informative for geographical relationships and the history of the rise and fall of states. Osprey books are often useful, but vary in reliability.

COMPETITION PERIODS

Some competition organizers prefer to limit armies to a specific historical time period, to minimize the culture shock arising from the clash of wildly anachronistic armies. At first sight, the breakdown of this series of army lists into the following four books might appear eminently suitable.

BOOK 1:	THE CHARIOT PERIOD	3000 BC - 500 BC.
BOOK 2:	THE CLASSICAL PERIOD	500 BC - 476 AD.
BOOK 3:	THE EARLY MEDIEVAL PERIOD	476 AD - 1071 AD.
BOOK 4:	THE HIGH MEDIEVAL PERIOD	1071 AD - 1525 AD.

Note however that some armies continue after the nominal period of the book in which they appear, so that division by books could unjustly prevent them from competing against actual historical opponents. Organizers should therefore subdivide competitions by the periods of the books, not by the books themselves. Obviously an army whose list crosses such a sub-period boundary can only use troops permitted it during the sub-period in which it is competing. If division into historical periods is not practicable, the initial pairings of a competition should try to match armies of similar date and geographical region, giving priority to the natural enemies listed.

1. EARLY SUMERIAN 3000 BC - 2334 BC and GREAT REVOLT c. 2250 BC

Dry. Ag 2. WW or DH, RH if DH, Rv, GH, O, E, SF, M, Rd, BUAf.
E: 1/1, 1/4, 1/5, 1/6, 1/9, 1/11.

C-in-C - Reg Bd (F) @ 26AP	1
Sub-generals - as above	0-2
Ally-general - Reg Bd (F) @ 16AP	0-2
Household and militia archers - Reg Bw (I) @ 4AP	36-96
Archers, settled or nomadic levy skirmishers - Irr Ps (O) @ 2AP	0-12
Javelinmen, settled or nomadic levy skirmishers - Irr Ps (I) @ 1AP	4-12
Slingers, settled or nomadic levy skirmishers - Irr Ps (O) @ 2AP	4-24
Camp - Reg Bge (O) @ 3AP, or pack-donkeys - Reg Bge (I) @ 2AP	0-2 per general
Ma - Irr Bts (O) @ 2AP [Any foot]	0-6
Dry steppe nomad allies - List: Early Bedouin (Bk 1/6)	
Zagros highlander allies - List: Zagros and Anatolian Highlanders (Bk 1/4)	
Elamite allies or vassals - List: Early Susiana and Elam (Bk 1/5)	

Only after 2800 BC:

Upgrade C-in-C or sub-general in 4-wheeled battle car to Reg Kn (I) @ 29AP, or on platform- or straddle-car to Reg Cv (I) @ 25AP, or on foot to Reg Pk (I) @ 23AP	Any
Upgrade ally-general as above, to Reg Kn (I) @ 19AP or Reg Cv (I) @ 15AP	Any
4-wheeled battle-cars - Irr Kn (I) @ 7AP	4-9
Scouts riding platform- or straddle-cars - Reg Cv (I) @ 5AP	0-1
Scouts riding asses - Irr LH (I) @ 3AP	0-2
Re-arm household and militia above as spearmen - Reg Pk (I) @ 3AP	All
Household and militia archers - Reg Ps (O) @ 2AP or Reg Bw (I) @ 4AP	4-6

Only if after 2800 BC and in a Kish C-in-C's own command:

Re-arm household spearmen as axemen - Reg Bd (F) @ 6AP	4-9

Only Kish in 2700 BC:

Upgrade C-in-C to Brilliant (as Agga of Kish) at 25AP extra	0 or 1

Only after 2500 BC:

Upgrade C-in-C or sub-general on foot to Reg Pk (X) @ 24AP	Any
Upgrade ally-general on foot to Reg Pk (X) @ 14AP	Any
Upgrade spearmen to Reg Pk (X) @ 4AP as front rank with body shields and shieldbearers	0-½
Syrian city-state allies - List: Early Syrian (Bk 1/9)	

Only after 2500 BC and if command's general is from Umma or Apishal:

Upgrade javelinmen to Martu bedouin mercenaries - Irr Ax (O) @ 3AP	0-6

Only the "Great Revolt" circa 2250 BC:

Levies and emergency reserves - Irr Hd (O) @ 1AP	8-21
Melukhkhan allies - List: Melukhkhan and Pre-Vedic Indian (Bk 1/10)	

This list covers the earliest attested Sumerian armies from the final stages of early state formation in southern Mesopotamia around the lower Tigris and Euphrates during the prehistoric Late Uruk period, until the accession of Sargon of Akkad and the creation of the first historical empire. Sumerian cultural and political colonisation had earlier been considerable, extending to Anatolia, Egypt, the Gulf, Syria, the Persian highlands and the Transcaucasus, but by the start of our period most colonies had been abandoned and inter-city warfare was endemic. Cities were surrounded by enormous thick mud-brick walls and included large palaces and temples. Society was highly stratified and wealth concentrated in the hands of the kings and religious hierarchy. Wars were thought of as between rival cities' gods, with the armies as their teams. A sub-general belongs to the same city state as the C-in-C; each ally-general represents a different city state. City organisation and army supply were controlled by the literate temple bureaucracy. Archaic proto-cuneiform texts of the late 4th millennium seem to list large bodies of archers under military officers, possibly the first regular army. By 2800 BC, the bulk of a Sumerian army was close order foot with long spears held in both hands. These initially lacked shields, relying instead on a leather or thick felt cape, studded with copper discs and probably dyed red or green if leather, left buff or off-white if felt. From about 2500 BC, large body shields were carried by separate shieldbearers armed only with a light axe, leaving the spearmen's hands free. In the "Vulture Stela" six rows of spearheads project in front of the shieldwall. In battle the

7

spearmen were preceded by skirmishers with bows, slings and javelins. The long dominant northern state of Kish used heavier broader-headed axes. Umma and Apishal used substantial numbers of Martu mercenaries after 2500 BC. Four-wheeled battle cars drawn by four expensive onager-donkey cross equids came into use around 2800 BC; and lighter platform-cars and straddle-cars may have been used as command and courier vehicles and for scouting. Battle-cars other than those of generals are classed as irregular because of their clumsiness. Recent research indicates that riding was more common this early than previously thought, but riding techniques were primitive and asses very inferior mounts to horses, so only a limited provision is made for mounted scouts. Nomadic levies represent temporarily resident and subject semi-nomadic pastoralists from the western steppe fringes or Lullubi, Guti or Hurrian highlanders from the Zagros mountains. The "Great Revolt" against Akkad immediately entered into Near Eastern mythology following Naram-Suen's astounding victory after 9 epic battles in a single year. The options here represent both the southern coalition under Lugal-Anne of Ur and the northern coalition under Ipkhur-Kishi of Kish. The third rebel alliance appears in the Zagros Highlanders list.

2. EARLY EGYPTIAN 3000 BC - 1541 BC

Dry. Ag 1. O, E, Rd, BUAf.
Before 1645 BC: In Delta, **Rv,** M, otherwise **WW**, RF. From 1645 BC: **WW**, RF.
E: 1/2, 1/3, 1/6, 1/7, 1/9, 1/15, 1/17

C-in-C - Reg Bd (O) @ 27AP, or in litter - Reg Bge (S) @ 26AP	1
Sub-general - Reg Bd (O) @ 27AP	1-2
Archers - Reg Bw (I) @ 4AP	16-36
Marines, spearmen of the residence and menfat - Reg Bd (F) @ 6AP	4-36
Conscripts under local commanders - Irr Hd (O) @ 1AP	4-24
Javelinmen paired with quiver carriers - Reg Ps (S) @ 3AP	0-8
Medjay and other Nubian archers - Irr Ps (O) @ 2AP or Irr Bw (O) @ 4AP	4-12
Bedouin slingers - Irr Ps (O) @ 2AP	0-5
Libyan javelinmen and archers - up to ¼ Irr Ps (O) @ 2AP, rest Irr Ps (I) @ 1AP	0-8
Camp - Irr Bge (O) @ 2AP, or pack-donkeys - Irr Bge (I) @ 1AP	0-2 per general
Ahaw - Irr Bts (S) @ 3AP [Bw, Bd]	0-10

Only after 1690 BC:

Upgrade generals in chariots to Reg Cv (O) @ 27AP	Any

This list covers Egyptian armies of the Early Dynastic, Old (2686 BC to 2181 BC - the period of the pyramid builders) and Middle Kingdoms. From about 1645 BC onwards, the northern half of Egypt was occupied by the Hyksos, but the military system of the southern half probably remained unchanged until Khamose reformed the army and started driving the Hyksos out. Hereditary archers and menfat "shock troops" were supported by conscripts. The centre of the battle line would consist of massed close fighters in columns or deep lines, supported by massed archer formations. Archers and close combat troops formed up in separate bodies. The archers were to discharge a heavy volume of arrows in support of the close-combat troops, while themselves avoiding hand-to-hand fighting. Lighter troops such as javelinmen or tribal auxiliaries would form up on the flanks of the array. Javelinman and quiver carrier figures based together as a pair are classed as Ps (S) because of the extra javelins. Although generals were usually bowmen, and can be so represented, their bodyguards were axemen with large shields. WW represents the Nile, Rv the branches of its delta. A very elderly 14 ½ hand chariot horse was found sealed in the c. 1675 BC destruction layer of a fortress at Buhen.

3. NUBIAN 3000 BC - 1480 BC

Dry. Ag 1. **Rv**, GH, **SF**, G or M or D. Kush from 1645 BC, BUA, F.
E: 1/2, 1/3, 1/7, 1/22.

C-in-C - Irr Bw (O) @ 14AP	1
Sub-general - Irr Wb (F) @ 13AP or Irr Bw (O) @ 14AP	1-2
Warriors - Irr Wb (F) @ 3AP	0-24
Archers - Irr Ps (O) @ 2AP or Irr Bw (O) @ 4AP	60-162
Javelinmen - Irr Ps (I) @ 1AP	0-25
Camp - Irr Bge (O) @ 2AP, or pack-donkeys - Irr Bge (I) @ 1AP	0-2 per general
Dugouts - Irr Bts (I) @ 1AP [Wb or Ps]	0-2

Only in 2310 BC:

Egyptian allies - List: Early Egyptian (Bk 1/2)	

Only Kush from 1645 BC to 1480 BC:

Scouts - Irr LH (I) @ 3AP	0-1
Egyptian mercenaries - up to ¼ Reg Bd (F) @ 6AP, rest Reg Bw (I) @ 4AP	0-8

This list covers Egypt's black neighbours south of the 1st Nile cataract until the conquest of Kush by the first three Pharaohs of the Egyptian 18th dynasty. They were predominantly archers, whose superior skills made them welcome in Egypt as mercenaries if not as tourists! Pharaoh Senusret III complained that they would not meet him in open battle, but withdrew when he attacked and attacked when he withdrew. Although they lived on the Nile, which beyond the cataracts is classed as a river rather than a waterway since it is accessible only with great difficulty to large vessels, they made little use of boats at this time. However, Egyptian forts were established on the cataracts with specific orders to prevent the passage of Nubian boats. After the collapse of the Middle Kingdom, remnant Egyptian garrisons in Nubia were taken over by the partly Egyptianised kings of Kush/Kerma. Although Kush was allied to the Hyksos, their armies never fought together.

4. ZAGROS AND ANATOLIAN HIGHLANDERS 3000 BC - 950 BC

Zagros Dry, others Cold. Ag 3. Rv, **DH**, RH, GH, O. E, Wd, BF in Cold, SF in Dry, Rd, BUA.
E: 1/1, 1/4, 1/5, 1/9, 1/11, 1/12, 1/15, 1/16, 1/19, 1/20, 1/21, 1/24, 1/25, 1/28, 1/31.

C-in-C - Irr Bd (F) @ 15AP or Irr Bw (O) @ 14AP	1
Sub-general - as above	0-1
Ally-general of same nation - Irr Bd (F) @ 10AP or Irr Bw (O) @ 9AP	0-3
Bodyguards - Irr Bd (F) @ 5AP or Irr Bw (O) @ 4AP	4-9
Warriors with javelin - Irr Ax (I) @ 2AP	24-120
Skirmishers with javelin or throwstick - Irr Ps (I) @ 1AP	16-30
Archers - Irr Ps (O) @ 2AP or Irr Bw (I) @ 3AP	24-72
Slingers - Irr Ps (O) @ 2AP	8-30
Camp - Irr Bge (O) @ 2AP, or pack-donkeys - Irr Bge (I) @ 1AP	0-2 per general

Only Guti from 2250 BC to 2194 BC:

Upgrade C-in-C in platform- or straddle-car to Irr Cv (I) @ 14AP	0-1

Only if Guti or Lullubi from 2250 BC to 2112 BC:

Upgrade warriors to Irr Wb (F) @ 3AP	Any

Only Guti in the Great Revolt of 2250 BC:

Anatolian allies - List: Zagros and Anatolian Highlanders (Bk 1/4)	
Mariote allies - List: Early Syrian (Bk 1/9)	
Elamite allies - List: Early Susiana and Elam (Bk 1/5)	
Markhashian archers - Irr Bw (I) @ 3AP	0-12
Melukhkhan men-at-arms - Reg Pk (F) @ 4AP or Reg Bd (F) @ 6AP	0-3
Melukhkhan archers - Reg Bw (O) @ 4AP	0-6
Makkanite warriors - up to ½ Irr Bd (F) @ 5AP, rest Irr Ax (I) @ 2AP	0-12
Black ships - Irr Shp (O) @ 3AP [Any Melukhkhans or Makkanites]	0-4

Only Guti from 2193 BC to 2112 BC:

Upgrade C-in-C riding platform- or straddle-car to Irr Cv (I) @ 14AP	1
Sumero-Akkadian militia spearmen - Reg Pk (F) @ 4AP or Reg Pk, up to half (X) @ 4AP, remainder (I) @ 3AP	12-30
Boats - Irr Bts (I) @ 1AP [any foot]	0-4
Subject Sumero-Akkadian city-state allies - List: Akkadian [but not Third Dynasty of Ur] (Bk 1/11)	

Only Gasgans:

Downgrade generals and bodyguards to Irr Wb (F) @ 13AP if C-in-C or sub-general, 8AP if ally-general, 3AP if not	Any
Upgrade warriors to Irr Wb (F) @ 3AP	½ -all

Only Hurrians after 1780 BC, or Early Kassites, Gasgans, Nairi lands or similar after 1650 BC:

Upgrade generals in 2-horse 2-crew chariots to Irr Cv (O) @ 16AP if C-in-C or sub-general, 11AP if ally-general	Any
Replace bodyguards by 2-horse 2-crew chariots - Irr Cv (O) @ 6AP	0-2

This list covers early upland peoples from the Zagros mountains, including Guti, Lullubi and early Kassites; and also of the wider highland horizon of the ancient Near East, including the early Hurrian highland states of north-eastern Mesopotamia, early Anatolian highlanders such as the Gasgans/Kashgans/Kaska, proto-Phrygians from their first arrival in western Asia Minor around 1200 BC until the founding of the Phrygian kingdom, and others too numerous to list. Generals and their bodyguards were armed with both composite bow and heavy axe.

The Great Revolt option represents the alliance against Akkad organised by Gula-an, King of Gutium. Whether the Elamites were involved is now thought doubtful, since while they were recorded as enemies by the King of Akkad, this appears to be at some later time. After the collapse of the Akkadian empire, the Guti dominated Mesopotamia for about a century. The Gasgans were perennial and feared foes of the Hittites. They seem to have had two classes of warriors, an elite and a supplementary force. The Guti and Lullubi were depicted without shields, but were used to frighten children and the latter said to have scorpion tails, possibly justifying an optional upgrade to Wb (F).

5. EARLY SUSIANA AND ELAM 3000 BC - 800 BC

Dry. Ag 3. Rv, DH, RH, GH, O, Wd, E, SF, RF, G, Rd, BUA.
E: 1/1, 1/4, 1/10, 1/11, 1/12, 1/15, 1/19, 1/21, 1/23, 1/25, 1/37, 1/41.

C-in-C - Irr Bw (O) @ 14AP	1
Sub-general - as C-in-C	0-1
Ally-general of same nation - Irr Bw (O) @ 9AP	0-3
Archers - Irr Bw (I) @ 3AP or Irr Ps (O) @ 2AP	56-150
Camp - Irr Bge (O) @ 2AP, or pack-donkeys - Irr Bge (I) @ 1AP	0-2 per general
Zagros highlander allies - List: Zagros and Anatolian Highlanders (Bk 1/4)	

Only from 2600 BC to 2300 BC:

Upgrade C-in-C or sub-general in 4-wheeled battle-car to Reg Kn (I) @ 29AP, or riding platform- or straddle-car to Reg Cv (I) @ 25AP, or on foot to Reg Bw (O) @ 25AP or Reg Bd (F) @ 26AP	All
Upgrade ally-general in 4-wheeled battle-car to Reg Kn (I) @ 19AP, or riding platform- or straddle-car to Reg Cv (I) @ 15AP, or on foot to Reg Bw (O) @ 15AP or Reg Bd (F) @ 16AP	Any
4-wheeled battle-cars - Irr Kn (I) @ 8AP	0-6

Only from 2600 BC to 2100 BC:

Household retinue - Reg Bd (F) @ 6AP or Reg Pk (F) @ 4AP	0-6
Household spearmen - Reg Pk, up to half (X) @ 4AP, remainder (I) @ 3AP	0-12
Upgrade archers to household and other retained archers - Reg Bw (I) @ 4AP	0-12

Only from 2600 BC to 1500 BC:

Scouts on platform- or straddle-cars - Reg Cv (I) @ 5AP	0-2

Only from 2600 BC to 1400 BC:

Scouts riding asses or other equids - Irr LH (I) @ 3AP	0-2

Only from 2300 BC to 1400 BC:

Upgrade C-in-C or sub-general riding platform- or straddle-car to Reg Cv (I) @ 25AP, or on foot to Reg Bw (O) @ 25AP or Reg Bd (F) @ 26AP	All
Upgrade ally-general riding platform- or straddle-car to Reg Cv (I) @ 15AP, or on foot to Reg Bw (O) @ 15AP or Reg Bd (F) @ 16AP	Any

Only from 2100 BC to 1850 BC:

Amurru allies - List: Early Bedouin (Bk 1/6)	
Melukhkhan allies - List: Melukhkhan and Pre-Vedic Indian (Bk 1/10.)	

Only from 2100 BC to 1600 BC:

Household retinue - Reg Bw (O) @ 5AP or Reg Bd (F) @ 6AP	0-12

Only in 1769 BC:

Mari allies - List: Later Amorite (Bk 1/15)	
Babylonian allies - List: Later Amorite (Bk 1/15)	

Only in 1768 BC:

Eshnunnan vassal allies - List: Sumerian Successor States (Bk 1/12)	

Only in 1764 BC:

Assyrian allies - List: Later Amorite (Bk 1/15)	
Eshnunnan allies - List: Sumerian Successor States (Bk 1/12)	
Malgi (Ammuru) allies - List: Early Bedouin (Bk 1/6)	

Only after 1400 BC:

Upgrade C-in-C in 2-horse 2-crew chariot to Reg Cv (O) @ 27AP or Reg Cv (S) @ 29AP	1
Upgrade ally-general in 2-horse 2-crew chariot to Reg Cv (O) @ 17AP or Reg Cv (S) @ 19AP	Any
Chariots - Reg Cv (S) @ 9AP or Reg Cv (O) @ 7AP	4-6
Chariots - Irr Cv (O) @ 6AP	4-8
Scouts riding horses - Irr LH (I) @ 3AP	0-2

This list covers the prehistoric proto-Elamite states east of Mesopotamia; including those of the lowland plain of Susiana until around 2700 BC, the later state of Elam and Anshan until the Shutrukids and their successors, eastern highland kingdoms such as Markhashi (located around Fars), Awan and Aratta, and the semi-nomadic cultures of trans-Elamite Bactria and Margiana circa 2500 - 1800 BC. Early Susiana and Elam either inspired or adopted many aspects of early Mesopotamian civilisation, but ultimately do not appear to have evolved into the Mesopotamian type of highly-organised centralised state. Elam was, however, a serious and perennial threat to its western neighbours when strong, and a tempting area for conquest when weak.

6. EARLY BEDOUIN 3000 BC - 312 BC

Dry. Ag 3. DH, RH, GH, Oa, SF, D or G. Martu only, CH, **DH**. Martu and Aramaeans only, BUA, F.
E: 1/1, 1/2, 1/6, 1/8, 1/9, 1/11, 1/12, 1/15, 1/17, 1/19, 1/20, 1/21, 1/22, 1/24, 1/25, 1/27, 1/29, 1/31, 1/34, 1/38, 1/44, 1/45, 1/46, 1/51, 1/52, 1/60, 2/7, 2/12, 2/16, 2/19.

C-in-C - Irr Ax (O) @ 13AP or Irr Wb (F) @ 13AP	1
Sub-general - as above	0-1
Bedouin ally-general - Irr Ax (O) @ 8AP or Irr Wb (F) @ 8AP	1-2
Javelinmen - Irr Ax (I) @ 2AP	40-150
Skirmishers with javelin - Irr Ps (I) @ 1AP	4-40
Slingers - Irr Ps (O) @ 2AP	4-20
Archers - Irr Ps (O) @ 2AP or Irr Bw (I) @ 3AP	4-20
Ass-riding scouts - Irr LH (I) @ 3AP	0-1
Camp - Irr Bge (O) @ 2AP, or pack-donkeys - Irr Bge (I) @ 1AP	0-2 per general

Only from 3000 BC to 1000 BC:

Upgrade archers to Irr Bw (O) @ 4AP	Any

Only after 2800 BC:

Retainers - Irr Wb (F) @ 3AP	0, or 4-8
Upgrade Ax javelinmen as shielded to Irr Ax (O) @ 3AP	Up to ½

Only from 2200 BC to 1894 BC:

Subject Syrian city allies - List: Early Syrian (Bk 1/9)	

Only Amurru from 2200 BC to 2000 BC:

Upgrade C-in-C or sub-general in 4-wheeled battle car to Reg Kn (I) @ 29AP, or on platform- or straddle-car to Reg Cv (I) @ 25AP, or on foot to Reg Pk (I) @ 23AP	Any
Upgrade ally-general as above, to Reg Kn (I) @ 19AP or Reg Cv (I) @ 15AP	Any

Only after 2100 BC:

Upgrade Ax javelinmen as shielded to Irr Ax (O) @ 3AP	½-all
Upgrade Ps javelinmen as shielded to Irr Ps (S) @ 3AP	0-3

Only from 2025 BC to 1800 BC:

Subject Mesopotamian city allies - List: Akkadian and Third Dynasty of Ur (Bk 1/11) or Sumerian Successor States (Bk 1/12)	

Only Hapiru, Sutu or Early Aramaeans from 2000 BC to 747 BC:

Upgrade C-in-C or sub-general in 2-horse 2-crew chariots to Irr Cv (O) @ 16AP	Any

Only Early Aramaeans from 2000 BC to 1101 BC:

Camel-riders - Irr Cm (O) @ 5AP or Irr LH (I) @ 3AP	1 per 4-6 Ax (O)
Archers - Irr Ps (O) @ 2AP [can support Ax (O)]	0-1 per 2 Ax (O)

Only Midianites and Amalekites from 1500 BC to 1000 BC and early Arabs from 1000 BC:

Upgrade generals to Irr Cm (O) @ 15AP if C-in-C or sub-general, 10AP if ally-general	All
Camelry - Irr Cm (O) @ 5AP	8-72
Replace ass-riding scouts with camel-mounted scouts - Irr LH (I) @ 3AP	All
Replace Bge (I) pack-donkeys with baggage-camels - Irr Bge (F) @ 2AP	All/0

Only early Arabs from 745 BC to 609 BC:

Provide archers with line of kneeling camels as barricade - PO @ 1AP	Any

This list covers all near-eastern desert or dry steppe nomads and semi-nomads prior to the widespread introduction of the ridden horse. It includes the Aamu ("He does not announce the day of fighting"), the pre-camel Amurru (also known as Martu or Amorites) originating in Syria as dry-steppe nomads, but by 2000 mostly living in villages as pastoralists or farmers, their later sub-groups such as the Sutu and Hanu, Early Aramaean nomads in Babylonia from 2000 BC, and major users of camels such as the Midianites and Amalekites, and early Arabs such as the Isamme, Nabaitayai, Kidraya and Atarsaman.

The usual method of fighting on foot, at least in single combat, was to shoot a few missiles then charge with hand weapons. The troops classed as Camelry (O) are depicted in Assyrian reliefs as having two archers mounted on each camel. This may not have been universal practice, since the Assyrians' war of attrition against them may have resulted in a temporary shortage of camels, necessitating doubling up. Whether one or two riders are depicted does not affect classification. Other Assyrian reliefs show archers fighting from behind a line of kneeling camels, hence the option for PO. Allied contingents supplied to other nations can disregard foot minima unless any foot are included or the total number of elements in the contingent exceeds 12 including baggage. All troops in this list count as bedouin.

7. EARLY LIBYAN 3000 BC - 70 AD

Dry. Ag 2 until 1292 BC, then Ag 4 until 665 BC, then Ag 1. S, Oa, **RF**, SF, G, D. After 400 BC, BUAf, F.
E: 1/2, 1/3, 1/17, 1/22, 1/28, 1/35, 1/46, 1/52, 1/53, 1/56, 1/60, 1/61, 2/7, 2/20, 2/32, 2/40, 2/49, 2/56.

C-in-C - Irr Wb (F) @ 13AP or Ax (I) @ 12AP	1
Sub-general - Irr Ps (I) @ 11AP or Ax (I) @ 12AP	1-2
Bodyguard swordsmen - Irr Wb (F) @ 3AP	0-3
Skirmishers with javelins, throwing sticks and clubs - Irr Ps (I) @ 1AP	40-108
Warriors with javelins, throwing sticks and clubs - all Irr Ax (I) @ 2AP or all Irr Hd (S) @ 2AP	48-144
Archers - Irr Ps (O) @ 2AP	0-18
Camp - Irr Bge (O) @ 2AP, or pack-donkeys or cattle herds - Irr Bge (I) @ 1AP	0-2 per general
Only from 2160 BC:	
Replace Ps (I) with archers - Irr Ps (O) @ 2AP or Irr Bw (I) @ 3AP	¼-½
Only from 1250 BC to 665 BC:	
Upgrade C-in-C to Irr Cv (O) in 2-horse chariot @ 16AP	1
2-horse chariots - Irr Cv (O) @ 6AP	1-6
Only from 1208 BC to 1180 BC:	
Sea Peoples mercenaries - Irr Bd (O) @ 5AP	0-6
Only from 1208 BC to 665 BC:	
Upgrade sub-generals to swordsmen - Irr Wb (F) @ 13AP	All
Upgrade warriors to swordsmen - Irr Wb (F) @ 3AP	0-60
Only in 1179 BC:	
Sea Peoples allies - List: Sea Peoples (Bk 1/28)	
Only after 665 BC:	
Upgrade generals to Irr Cv (O) in 4-horse chariots @ 16AP	All
4-horse chariots - Irr Cv (O) @ 6AP	2-8
Replace Wb, Ax (I) and Hd (S) with spearmen using large hide shield - Irr Sp (I) @ 3AP.	All/0
Only Garamantes from 500 BC to 70 AD:	
Replace 4-horse chariots by cavalry - Irr LH (O) @ 14AP if general, otherwise 4AP	Any
Replace spearmen with javelinmen using small shield - Irr Ax (O) @ 3AP	All
Replace Ps (I) with archers - Irr Ps (O) @ 2AP	All
War dogs - Irr Wb (F) @ 2AP	0-4

This list covers all independent Libyan armies based beyond the western borders of Egypt until the conquest of the Garamantes by the Romans. Libyan armies are described as fighting by skirmishing, ambush and massed wave assaults. They were initially entirely of foot lacking shields and armed with javelins, throwing sticks/clubs and a few bows, but these traditional weapons were later supplemented first by an increase in bow use, then by the import of limited quantities of chariots from Egypt and then of "sea people" bronze thrusting swords. They were at first a perennial nuisance, raiding, then retreating into the stony border desert using heat, thirst, distance, harassment and ambush to defeat pursuit or punitive expeditions. Towards the end of the New Kingdom they began to attack Egypt in such strength that the Egyptians were unable to prevent large scale settlement. Their threat was especially severe when combined with the attacks of the Sea Peoples from 1208 BC to 1176 BC. By this time they had differentiated into the more traditionalist Libu, and the bow, sword and chariot using Meshwesh, but even the former used archers, swordsmen and foreign troops against Merenptah. The process is partly concealed, as it is suspected that Egyptian representations of Libyans after the Old Kingdom are symbolic and may not represent their contemporary appearance. Large scale invasions involved confederate armies commanded by either a Meshwesh or a Libu paramount chief.

Herodotos describes the Libyan contingent in Xerxes army in 480 BC as dressed in goat skins, armed only with fire-hardened wooden javelins and as using chariots. Several 6[th]century Persian monuments depict a long unbelted garment and a probably hide cloak. One man has 2 metal-headed javelins slung from his neck and no shield. The earlier 2-horse chariots were Egyptian-pattern, but the later 4-horse chariots were apparently based on 7th and 6th century Near Eastern styles, but with unarmoured horses and crewed by unarmoured javelinmen. The town-dwelling Garamantes of the Fezzan area of central inland Libya used underground irrigation channels fed by fossil water from deep wells, had an Egyptian-style religion and even built small mud-brick pyramids. They are recorded by Herodotos as using chariots and these are depicted in rock art, but Strabo writing around 25 AD does not mention them and one graffito depicts a Garamantean horseman holding what might be a small shield. Very early rock art depicts Garamanteans as a minority of javelinmen in long garments with small shields plus a majority of archers and also shows chariots. Strabo (describing Moors, but also including other Libyans) says they were long ungirded tunics with a wide border and leopard or lion-skin cloaks, and also refers to elephant-hide shields; "aspides" (large shields) for the foot and pelta (small shields) for horsemen. Since the Carthaginians got their elephants from Mauretania and Numidia, these are not likely to have been available on the borders of Egypt. At Krimisos in 341 BC, probable Libyans in Carthaginian service were indistinguishable at a distance from the hoplite phalanx, which implies they fought as close order spearmen. Pliny remarks on the Garamantes' use of war dogs, introduced at an unspecified date by an exiled king to help in his restoration.

8. MAKKAN, DILMUN, SABA, MA'IN AND QATABAN 2800 BC - 312 BC

Dry. Ag 1. S. **DH**, RH, O, Wd, E, SF, BUAf.
E: 1/6, 1/8, 1/10, 1/11, 1/60,

C-in-C- Irr Bd (F) @ 15AP	1
Sub-general - Irr Bd (F) @ 15AP	0-1
Ally-general of same nation - Irr Bd (F) @ 10AP	1-3
Scouts riding equids - Irr LH (I) @ 3AP	0-2
Warriors - Irr Ax (I) @ 2AP	28-120
Upgrade warriors to Irr Bd (F) @ 5AP	Up to ¼
Skirmishers with bow - Irr Ps (O) @ 2AP	4-30
Skirmishers with javelin - Irr Ps (I) @ 1AP	12-24
Camp - Irr Bge (O) @ 2AP, or pack-donkeys - Irr Bge (I) @ 1AP	0-2 per general

Only from 2000 BC:

Upgrade warriors with shield to Irr Ax (O) @ 3AP	Any
Upgrade javelin skirmishers with shield to Irr Ps (S) @ 3AP	Any

Only from 2000 BC to 1900 BC:

Melukhkhan "men-at-arms" - Reg Pk (F) @ 4AP or Reg Bd (F) @ 6AP	0-2
Melukhkhan or Black ships - Irr Shp (O) @ 3AP [Bd, Ax, Ps]	0-4

Only if Makkan after 1300 BC:

Change C-in-C to Irr Wb (F) @ 13AP	1
Change sub-general to Irr Wb (F) @ 13AP	All
Change ally-general to Irr Wb (F) @ 8AP	All
Upgrade warriors to Irr Wb (F) @ 3AP	All
Archers - Irr Bw (I) @ 3AP	24-60

Only if Dilmun from 1300 BC to 1000 BC:

Babylonian allies - List: Kassite and Later Babylonian (Bk 1/21)	

Only after 1000 BC:

Upgrade generals to Irr Cv (I) @ 15 AP if C-in-C or sub-general, 10 AP if ally-general	Any
Cavalry - Irr Cv (I) @ 5AP	2-4
Upgrade warriors with camels to Irr Cm (O) @ 5AP	0-16
Change scouts to camel-mounted - Irr LH (I) @ 3AP	Any
Upgrade Bge (I) to pack-camels - Irr Bge (F) @ 2AP	All/0

Only if Saba, Ma'in or Qataban after 700 BC:

Central Arabian allies - List: Early Bedouin (Bk 1/6)	

This list covers armies of the resource-rich kingdoms of the eastern seaboard of Arabia (then known as Makkan and probably centred on the modern Sultanate of Oman), the related ancient maritime state of Dilmun (probably extending from Failaka to the Qatar peninsula and centred on northern Bahrain), and the large agricultural kingdoms of the Yemen, primarily Saba (Biblical Sheba) and Ma'in, but also their vassals and ex-vassals of Qataban, Hadramaut and Himyar. Dilmun at its height functioned as the premier trading emporium in the Gulf and the hub of an international long-distance commercial network which linked Mesopotamia to Melukhkha (the Indus valley), and eastern Iran via Makkan. The Gulf had been in trading contact with Mesopotamia and Iran from at least the 5th millennium BC, with especially strong influences from the Harappan culture of the Indus valley around 2000 BC. Kings of the dynasty of Akkad campaigned in, and possibly conquered, Makkan. Akkadian texts show that large armies were coalitions of dozens of small kingdoms, possibly under an identifiable overlord like the King Manium captured by Naram-Suen.

The typical, though mostly unpublished, weaponry of circa 2800 BC - 1800 BC consists of large well-made copper slashing swords (of varying lengths but generally similar to the sea-people's type) supplemented with a variety of missile weapons and daggers. Similarities with later Indian weaponry are intriguing in view of Makkan's close contact with the Harappans. Oasis towns were guarded by numbers of massive stone and brick towers built around central wells. The Gulf kingdoms' sea power was essentially mercantile, hence the absence of local ships in this list. Melukhkhan ships can carry troops of other origin.

9. EARLY SYRIAN 2700 BC - 2200 BC

Dry if Mari, otherwise Warm. Ag 2. S, Rv, GH, DH, O, E, SF & RH in Dry, RF & SH in Warm, Rd, BUAf, D.
E: 1/1, 1/2, 1/4, 1/6, 1/9, 1/11.

C-in-C: in 4-wheeled battle-car - Reg Kn (I) @ 29AP, or riding platform- or straddle-car - Reg Cv (I) @ 25AP, or on foot - Reg Pk (I) @ 23AP or Reg Pk (X) @ 24AP, or Reg Bd (F) @ 26AP	1
Sub-general - as above	0-1
Ally-general: in 4-wheeled battle-car - Reg Kn (I) @ 19AP, or riding platform- or straddle-car - Reg Cv (I) @ 15AP, or on foot - Reg Pk (I) @ 13AP or Reg Pk (X) @ 14AP or Reg Bd (F) @ 16AP	1-2
Battle-cars - Irr Kn (I) @ 7AP	0-4
Scouts mounted on equids - Irr LH (I) @ 3AP	0-1
Household and militia spearmen - up to ½ Reg Pk (X) @ 4AP, remainder Reg Pk (I) @ 3AP	4-24
Upgrade Reg Pk (I) household spearmen to axemen - Reg Bd (F) @ 6AP	0-8
Fully equipped household or militia archers - Reg Bw (I) @ 4AP	4-8
Settled, nomadic levy or militia slingers - Irr Ps (O) @ 2AP	0-36
Settled, nomadic levy or militia archers - Irr Ps (O) @ 2AP or Irr Bw (I) @ 3AP	36-48
Settled, nomadic levy or militia javelinmen: up to ½ shielded - Irr Ax (O) @ 3AP, remainder unshielded - Irr Ax (I) @ 2AP or Irr Ps (I) @ 1AP	24-72
Camp - Irr Bge (O) @ 2AP, or pack-donkeys - Irr Bge (I) @ 1AP	0-2 per general
Ma-gur - Irr Bts (S) @ 3AP [Pk, Bw]	0-2
Sumerian city-state allies or subject-allies - List: Early Sumerian (Bk 1/1)	
Dry steppe nomad allies - List: Early Bedouin (Bk 1/6)	

This list represents the culturally Sumerian early Syrian states such as Mari and Ebla before they were over-run by the Amurru. It also covers Syrian subject allies of the Amurru between 2200 BC and 1894 BC. Both fully equipped and irregular archers are well-attested for Syrian forces of this period. Although archers are shown at sieges protected by pavise-bearing spearmen, this is not so for battle in the field. No more than 20 elements can be nomadic levy classed as Bedouin. Mari vied with Kish and Akshak for control of northern Babylonia. Correspondence survives between the kings of Mari and Ebla in which the former surveys all their wars of the past 100 years and wearily warns Ebla not to try it again!

10. MELUKHKHAN AND PRE-VEDIC INDIAN 2700 BC - 1500 BC

Tropical. Ag 0. S, Rv, **Wd**, E, SF, M, Rd, BUAf.
E: 1/5, 1/8, 1/10, 1/11, 1/23.

C-in-C - Reg Pk (F) @ 24AP	1
Sub-general - as above	1-2
Spearmen - Reg Pk (F) @ 4AP or Reg Sp (I) @ 4AP	8-48
Archers - Reg Bw (I) @ 4AP	12-60
Kulli highlanders - Irr Ax (I) @ 2AP	0-20
Peasant slingers - Irr Ps (O) @ 2AP	28-42
Camp - Irr Bge (O) @ 2AP, or laden ox-carts - Irr Bge (I) @ 1AP	0-2 per general

Only before 1900 BC:

Elephants - Irr El (O) @ 16AP	0-1
Scouts mounted on asses - Irr LH (I) @ 3AP	0-3
"Men-at-arms" - Reg Pk (F) @ 4AP or Reg Bd (F) @ 6AP	3-6
Melukhkhan or Black ships - Irr Shp (O) @ 3AP [men-at-arms]	0-6

The proto-Indian or Harappan civilisation of the Indus valley of western India was known to the Mesopotamians as the land of Melukhkha. Since Harappan hieroglyphs are as yet untranslated, we do not know their own name for themselves. Melukhkhans had a reputation as interpreters, merchants and seamen and provided forces for the Great Revolt against Akkad and for the enemies of the Third Dynasty of Ur. Their ships carried regular soldiers apparently similar to Mesopotamian guardsmen. Allied contingents can therefore include ships. The Indus civilisation collapsed c. 1900 BC, and was replaced by a less urbanised Pre-Vedic culture displaced by Aryan invaders around 1500 BC.

Troops are classed as regular by analogy with other contemporary city states. There is no direct evidence of mounted troops, but elephant and horse were domesticated, ox-carts with 2 and 4 solid wheels were in use, and there were trading contacts with Sumer, so a few war elephants, mounted scouts and/or battle cars cannot be ruled out, though the last seem very unlikely and are omitted here. Slingstones are very prominent in the archaeological record. Copper or bronze arrow points, spearheads (some barbed); short swords, daggers and axe heads and stone mace heads are also known. There is one possible representation on a seal of a rectangular shield, which would be incompatible with the garments depicted worn by the upper classes.

11. AKKADIAN 2334 BC - 2193 BC, AND THIRD DYNASTY OF UR 2112 BC - 2004 BC

Dry. Akkad: Ag 4. Third Dynasty of Ur: Ag 2. WW, Rv, GH, DH, RH, O, E, SF, M, Rd, BUAf. Only from 2059 BC: FW
E: 1/1, 1/4, 1/5, 1/6, 1/8, 1/9, 1/10, 1/11, 1/12.

Scouts on platform- or straddle-car - Reg Cv (I) @ 5AP	0-2
Scouts riding equids - Irr LH (I) @ 3AP	0-2
Household retinue - Reg Bd (F) @ 6AP	3-6
Household spearmen - Reg Pk (F) @ 4AP or Reg Pk, up to ½ (X) @ 4AP, remainder (I) @ 3AP	4-12
Household archers - Reg Bw (O) @ 5AP or Reg Ps (O) @ 2AP [Ps can support household spearmen]	0-6
Militia spearmen - Reg Pk, up to ½ (X) @ 4AP, remainder (I) @ 3AP	20-64
Levies and emergency reserves - Irr Hd (O) @ 1AP	0-20
Militia or settled/nomadic levy archers - Irr Ps (O) @ 2AP	8-12
Militia or settled/nomadic levy slingers - Irr Ps (O) @ 2AP	8-21
Militia or settled/nomadic levy javelinmen - Irr Ps (I) @ 1AP	8-12
Northern militia spearmen - Reg Pk (F) @ 4AP or Reg Pk (I) @ 3AP	0-6
Camp - Reg Bge (O) @ 3AP, or pack-donkeys - Reg Bge (I) @ 2AP	0-2 per general
Ditch and bank for camp - TF @ 1AP	0, or 1-2 per Bge (O)
Pits as field obstacles - FO @ 2AP	0-12

Only from 2334 BC to 2193 BC:

C-in-C: in 4-wheeled battle-car - Reg Kn (I) @ 29AP, or on platform- or straddle-car - Reg Cv (I) @ 25AP, or on foot - Reg Bd (F) @ 26AP	1
Sub-general - as above	0-3
4-wheeled battle-cars - Irr Kn (I) @ 7AP	0-3
Sumerian subject or unwilling allies - List: Early Sumerian (Bk 1/1)	
Elamite subject allies - List: Early Susiana and Elam (Bk 1/5)	
Syrian subject allies - List: Early Syrian (Bk 1/9)	

Only from 2334 BC to 2279 BC:

Upgrade C-in-C to Brilliant (as Sargon of Akkad) at 25AP extra	0 or 1

Only from 2278 BC:

Upgrade militia spearmen to Reg Pk (F) @ 4AP	Any
Lullubi, Guti or Hurri highlander levy javelinmen - Irr Ax (I) @ 2AP	0, or 4-12
Eastern highlander, Elamite or Markhashian archers - Irr Ps (O) @ 2AP or Irr Bw (I) @ 3AP	1-12

Only from 2254 BC to 2218 BC:

Upgrade C-in-C to Brilliant (as Naram-Suen of Akkad) at 25AP extra	0 or 1

Only before 2253 BC:

Amurru bedouin levies - Irr Ax (O) @ 3AP or Irr Ax (I) @ 2AP	0-3

Only from 2253 BC to 2193 BC:

Amurru bedouin levies: up to ½ shielded - Irr Ax (O) @ 3AP, remainder unshielded - Irr Ax (I) @ 2AP	0-18

Only the Third Dynasty of Ur from 2112 BC to 2004 BC:

C-in-C riding platform- or straddle-car - Reg Cv (I) @ 25AP, or on foot - Reg Bw (O) @ 25AP	1
Sub-general - as above	1-3
Frontier troops - up to ½ Reg Ps (S) @ 3AP or Reg Ax (O) @ 4AP, rest Reg Ps (I) @ 1AP or Reg Ax (I) @ 3AP	0-18
Amurru bedouin levies - Irr Ax (O) @ 3AP	0-18

Only the Third Dynasty of Ur after 2028 BC:

Downgrade sub-generals to ally-generals - Reg Cv (I) @ 15AP or Reg Bw (O) @ 15AP	All
Upgrade household or militia spearmen with Amorite shield to Reg Sp (I) @ 4AP	½ - all
Amurru allies - List: Early Bedouin (Bk 1/6)	

This list represents the armies of the Dynasty founded by Sargon of Akkad (the famed Sharru-kin), who became for all Mesopotamians the paradigm of a military conqueror, "The King of Battle", and the most illustrious and revered monarch of the ancient near east. If all the accounts of Sargon's exploits are true, as seems increasingly likely, Akkadian armies campaigned far beyond Mesopotamia into Syria, Cyprus and the Mediterranean, Anatolia, highland Iran, and down the Gulf to Oman. Although the Akkadian empire was racked by massive revolts, the army and its generals remained loyal throughout and generally victorious until Mesopotamia was over-run by the Guti and Lullubi.

The list also covers the "Sumerian Renaissance" armies of the Third Dynasty of Ur, which drove out the Guti and Lullubi, then achieved stability at the cost of an eventually stifling bureaucracy. The large rectangular shields of former times [often left behind in difficult terrain, hence the option for Pk (F)] were replaced towards the end of the dynasty by lighter and more manageable Amorite shields. Normal deployment was as a vanguard, a main body divided into two wings, and a rearguard, each with a sacred standard.

Peaceful Amurru bedouin settlement of Mesopotamia began around 2500 BC, but later accelerated into violent invasions following progressive desiccation of the Arabian-Syrian steppe. A frontier wall "the Amorite wall" kept them out for a time.

12. SUMERIAN SUCCESSOR STATES 2028 BC - 1460 BC

Isin and Sealand: Dry. Ag 2. WW, Rv, GH, O, E, SF, M (**M** if Sealand), Rd, BUAf.
Others: Dry. Ag 2. WW, Rv, GH, DH, RH, O, E, SF, M, Rd, BUAf.
E: 1/4, 1/5, 1/6, 1/11, 1/12, 1/15, 1/21.

C-in-C : on 4-equid platform-car - Reg Cv (I) @ 25AP, or on foot - Reg Bw (O) @ 25AP, or on horse or other equid - Reg Mtd Bw (O) @ 26AP	1
Sub-general - as above	1-2
4-equid platform-cars - Reg Cv (I) @ 5AP	0-3
Scouts riding equids - Irr LH (I) @ 3AP	0-2
Royal retinue - Reg Pk (F) @ 4AP or Reg Bd (F) @ 6AP or Reg Sp (O) @ 5AP	0, or 2--4
Royal archers - Reg Bw (O) @ 5AP	0-3
Militia spearmen - Reg Pk, up to ½ (X) @ 4AP, rest (I) @ 3AP, or all Reg Pk (F) @ 4AP, or all Reg Sp (I) @ 4AP	20-60
Militia archers - Reg Bw (I) @ 4AP or Reg Ps (O) @ 2AP	0-3
Skirmishers:	
- archers - Irr Ps (O) @ 2AP	4-12
- slingers - Irr Ps (O) @ 2AP	4-12
- javelinmen - Irr Ps (I) @ 1AP	4-12
Camp - Irr Bge (O) @ 2AP, or pack-donkeys - Irr Bge (I) @ 1AP	0-2 per general
Elamite mercenary archers - Irr Bw (I) @ 3AP or Irr Ps (O) @ 2AP	0-12
Zagros highlander or Turruku mercenary warriors - Irr Ax (I) @ 2AP	3-6
Zagros highlander mercenary archers - Irr Bw (I) @ 3AP	4-12
Only Eshnunna from 2028 BC to 1762 BC:	
Elamite allies - List: Early Susiana and Elam (Bk 1/5)	
Assyrian allies - List: Later Amorite (Bk 1/15)	
Only Isin from 2017 BC to 1794 BC:	
Amurru mercenary javelinmen - Irr Ax (O) @ 3AP	4-12
Amurru mercenary slingers or archers - Irr Ps (O) @ 2AP	2-8
Only Larsa from 2000 BC to 1762 BC:	
Amurru allies - List: Early Bedouin (Bk 1/6)	
Only after 2000 BC:	
Upgrade generals' vehicles (if any) to 2-horse 2-crew chariots - Reg Cv (O) @ 27AP	All
Only after 1760 BC:	
Replace other platform cars with 2-horse 2-crew chariots - Reg Cv (O) @ 7AP	All
Only Sealand from 1732 BC to 1460 BC:	
Reed boats - Irr Bts (I) @ 1AP [Ps]	0-6

This list covers the southern Mesopotamian successor kingdoms of the Isin-Larsa period following the collapse of the Third Dynasty of Ur, including Hurrian influenced Eshnunna 2028 BC - 1762 BC, Larsa 2025 BC - 1762 BC, and the First Dynasty of Isin 2017 BC - 1787 BC. All these kingdoms, but particularly Isin, appear to have preserved a more substantial element of "Sumerian" military tradition for a longer period than other Mesopotamian states, or the Amorite kingdoms of the west. Larsa was ruled by Amorite and Elamite dynasties, and Eshnunna was under strong Elamite and Hurrian influence in addition to its "Sumerian" military inheritance.

The list also covers the Dynasty of the Sealand 1732 BC - 1460 BC founded by Iluma-ilum (who claimed descent from the last king of Isin) in his revolt against Babylon. Centred on the otherwise unidentified city of Urukug in the marshes of Sumer, and controlling the trade on the lower Euphrates to the Gulf, it was a constant irritation and threat to the kings of Babylon for nearly 300 years. Its last king, Ea-gamil, was eventually defeated by the Kassite king Ulamburiash around 1460 BC. Up to 6 elements of Amurru mercenaries can count as Bedouin.

13. HSIA CHINESE 2000 BC - 1763 BC AND SHANG CHINESE 1750 BC - 1017 BC

Cool. Ag 3. WW, Rv, DH, SH, GH, Wd, BF, M, Rd, BUAf, F.
E: 1/13, 1/14, 1/32.

C-in-C - Reg Bd (F) @ 26AP or Reg Bw (O) @ 25AP	1
Sub-general - as above	0-1
Chinese ally-general - Irr Bd (F) @ 10AP, or Irr Bd (I) @ 9AP or Irr Bw (O) @ 9AP	1-3
Nobles - Irr Bw (O) @ 4AP	2-4
Dagger-axe men - Irr Bd (I) @ 4AP	24-120
Spearmen - Irr Ax (O) @ 3AP	0-24
Archers - Irr Bw (I) @ 3AP or Irr Ps (O) @ 2AP	8-48
Upgrade dagger-axe men to Reg Bd (I) @ 5AP, spearmen to Reg Ax (O) @ 4AP or archers to Reg Bw (I) @ 4AP or Reg Ps (O) @ 2AP	Up to ½ of each type
Elephants - Irr El (O) @ 16AP	0-1
Camp - Irr Bge (O) @ 2AP, or laden ox-wagons - Irr Bge (I) @ 1AP	0-2 per general
Dug-outs - Irr Bts (I) @ 1AP [Bd, Ax, Bw, Ps]	0-4
Jung or I allies - List: Early Northern Barbarians (Bk 1/14)	
Only Shang after 1300 BC:	
Replace generals and nobles with 3-man 2-horse chariots - Irr Cv (S) @ 13AP if ally-general, 18AP if other general, 8AP if not.	All
Convict/conscripted slave foot - Irr Hd (F) @ 1AP	0-12
War dogs - Irr Wb (F) @ 2AP	0-2
Only Shang after 1100 BC:	
Chou allies - List: Western Chou and Spring and Autumn Chinese (Bk 1/32)	
Only Shang from 1059 BC to 1027 BC:	
Downgrade C-in-C to Inert general (as Ti Hsin) @ 75AP less	

The Shang were the first truly historical Chinese dynasty. They traditionally replaced the earlier Hsia dynasty in 1763 BC, but archaeology suggests continuity with the Hsia, and the likelihood is that the two dynasties existed for a period alongside and influencing each other. It therefore seems reasonable to assume that the Hsia military system, of which we have no direct evidence, was very similar to that of the Shang which eventually replaced it. Shang society was based on the tsu, a lineage group which also served as a military unit. Most tsu troops seem to have been called up only for specific campaigns, but some levies formed a lu standing army and the others, the tsu headed by members of the royal family, were involved in expeditions on a regular basis. The option has therefore been provided to upgrade these to regular as permanently embodied troops. One Shang army is described as comprising 10,000 lu and 3,000 tsu troops. Society was highly stratified; and the nobles have been left as irregular on the assumption that such a social organisation does not encourage discipline among the aristocracy. The last Shang king was defeated and killed by the Chou in 1027, but his heir was retained as a Chou vassal and allied with Chou rebels in a revolt from 1019 to 1017.

Close-fighting infantry were armed with the short one-handed "ko" dagger-axe (which is the commonest weapon in graves) or a 5 foot long spear. Dagger-axe men are graded as (I) because of inadequate training and confidence, not because of their weapons. Shields were relatively flimsy constructions of wicker and hide and of moderate size. Although there are oracle-bone references to "many archers" and arrowheads seem common even in non-chariot graves, the actual numbers mentioned are in the low hundreds. The lay-out of grave groups at Anyang suggests that at least some infantry were mobile enough to co-operate closely with chariots.

It is now thought that all chariots had a crew of 3 like those of the ensuing Chou period. However, a Chinese source says that "Shang chariots were renowned for speed, but Chou for excellence", suggesting that the former were lighter and flimsier, hense the clsssification as Cv (S). The 3-man crew would consist of a driver, an archer and a short dagger-axe man (so not with a long weapon). Chariots may occasionally have had four horses.

The evidence for war elephants is tenuous, but elephant bones are known from Shang sites and the animals were certainly hunted and probably tamed, since the Shang ideograph for elephant is a stylised drawing of an elephant led by a man. Chinese mythology describes the legendary pre-Hsia kings taming and using elephants in war. If war elephants in fact existed, they would be of the Indian species. Slaves conscripted as shock-troops by the last Shang king either did not fight or quickly defected. Hd (F) seems more suitable for these than the Wb (F) usually used for Chinese convict troops.

21

14. EARLY NORTHERN BARBARIANS 2000 BC - 315 BC

Cool. North European Bronze Age before 1400 BC, Ag 0. Others, Ag 3.
Rv, GH, DH, SH, Wd, BF, BUA, F. If North European Bronze Age or Iron Age, also S, WW, BUAf, M, E.
E: 1/13, 1/14, 1/26, 1/32, 1/33, 1/43, 1/47, 2/4, 2/11

C-in-C - Irr Wb (S) @ 15AP or Irr Wb (F) @ 13AP	1
Sub-general - as above	1-2
Warriors - Irr Wb (F) @ 3AP	48-150
Archers and/or slingers - Irr Ps (O) @ 2AP	10-24
Unenthusiastic levies, families, slaves, ill-equipped raiders etc. - Irr Hd (O) @ 1AP	0-10
Camp - Irr Bge (O) @ 2AP, or laden ox-wagons - Irr Bge (I) @ 1AP	0-2 per general
Only North European Bronze Age before 1400 BC:	
Re-grade warriors as Irr Bw - up to ½ (O) @ 4AP, remainder (I) @ 3AP	All
Only North European Bronze Age from 1400 BC to 701 BC:	
Upgrade generals to Irr Cv (O) @ 16AP if in chariots, or Irr Bd (O) @ 15AP if on foot	All
Solar disk in sacred chariot - Irr Bge (S) @ 3AP	0-1
Upgrade warriors to armoured warriors - Irr Bd (O) @ 5AP	0-15
Upgrade remaining warriors to Irr Ax (S) @ 4AP	All
Only North European Bronze Age and Iron Age from 1400 BC to 315 BC:	
Horsemen - Irr Cv (I) @ 5AP	0-6
Replace archers with skirmishing javelinmen - Irr Ps (I) @ 1AP	0-6
Longboats - Irr Bts (O) @ 2AP [Any foot]	0-6
Only North European Iron Age from 700 BC to 315 BC:	
Upgrade generals in chariots to Irr Cv (O) @ 16AP, or on foot - Irr Wb (S) @ 15AP	1-3
Warriors in 2-horse 2-crew chariots - Irr Cv (O) @ 6AP, or on foot - Irr Wb (S) @ 5AP	4-12
Only Kuei-fang and Hsien-yun from 1100 BC - 800 BC:	
Upgrade generals in chariots: 2-crew - Irr Cv (S) @ 18AP or 3-crew - Irr Kn (O) @ 19AP	Any
Chariots - as generals, Irr Cv (S) @ 8AP or Irr Kn (O) @ 9AP	0-3
Only Red Ti, from 788 BC - 588 BC:	
Upgrade up to half warriors to Irr Wb (S) @ 5AP, and downgrade all other warriors to Irr Hd (O) @ 1AP	All/0
Hsing Chinese allies - List: Western Chou and Spring and Autumn Chinese (Bk 1/32)	
Only Jung:	
Upgrade Wb (F) as "leather coated warriors" to Irr Wb (O) @ 3AP	0-12
Only I:	
Replace Wb with extra archers - Irr Bw (I) @ 3AP or Irr Ps (O) @ 2AP	¼ to ½
Only Jung or Ch'iang after 400 BC:	
Convert generals to Irr LH (F) @ 14AP or Irr Cv (O) @ 17AP	Any
Horse archers - Irr LH (F) @ 4AP	0, or 8-24

This list covers the armies of the North European Bronze and Early Iron Age and the various tribal peoples of north China, referred to by the Chinese as Jung, Ti, I, Ch'iang and other names, from the beginnings of Chinese history to the last great Ch'in defeat of the western Jung in 315 BC, by which time most of these peoples had been absorbed by their Chinese neighbours.

Despite the chilling evidence from several sites of Neolithic bow warfare, the Early North European Bronze Age is conventionally thought to have been a prosperous time of organised theocratic states that spent their energy in constructing vast religious monuments such as Stonehenge, rather than in war. Its downfall seems to have been through over-population and climatic change. As conditions deteriorated, it has been postulated that the priest-kings relied for a time on mercenaries adding copper and later bronze axe and short sword/dagger to their bow (the Beaker culture?), before being succeeded by warrior-rulers who instead often constructed massive hill forts (BUAf on DH). Long spears (or at least spears with heavy heads) now became an important weapon, outnumbering swords 10 to 1, but do not seem to have been used in formation. The rich used bronze armour. Horsemen are depicted in hand-to-hand combat, so are classed as cavalry rather than light horse. The Iron Age brought an increased use of chariots in war and the near disappearance of the bow. The Hjortspring boat finds, dated to around 350 BC, suggest a crew of 4 men with mail, sword, spear and narrow shield and 18 with only spear, javelin and broad shield.

The Chinese tribes mostly, if not all, fought as infantry; but an early Western Chou inscription mentioning "vehicles" captured from the Kuei-fang has been interpreted as evidence for chariots, which are also illustrated on Mongolian rock-carvings; and at the end of the period, the Jung and Ch'iang may have started riding ponies. In 706 the states of Ch'i and Cheng defeated a Northern Jung army and took the heads of 300 of their leather-coated warriors (probably wearing the relatively clumsy Chinese armour denoted by the same word). The I of the Huai valley were famous archers and probably had more bowmen than the rest. They still seem to have been capable of independent action right through to the end of this period. The Red Ti seem to have been a group of aristocratic warrior clans, ruling over subjugated clans. They were for a while the most warlike and successful of the Ti groups; the Chinese allies represent the state of Hsing, coerced into joining a Red Ti campaign against Wei in 642 BC.

15. LATER AMORITE 1894 BC - 1595 BC

Babylonia: Dry. Ag 3. WW, Rv, GH, O, E, SF, M, Rd, BUAf.
Assyria: Dry. Ag 3. Rv, GH, DH, RH, O, Wd, E, SF, Rd, BUAf.
Others: Dry. Ag 2. WW, Rv, GH, DH, RH, O, E, SF, D, Rd, BUAf.
E: 1/2, 1/4, 1/5, 1/6, 1/12, 1/15, 1/16, 1/17, 1/19.

C-in-C: in 4-equid platform-car - Reg Cv (I) @ 25AP, or on foot, Reg Bw (O) @ 25AP, or on horse or other equid - Reg Mtd Bw (O) @ 26AP	1
Sub-general - as above	0-2
Ally-general:- in 4-equid platform-car - Reg Cv (I) @ 15AP, or on foot - Reg Bw (O) @ 15AP, or on horse or other equid - Reg Mtd Bw (O) @ 16AP	1-2
2-horse 2-man chariots - Reg Cv (O) @ 7AP	0-2
Scouts riding horses or other equids - Irr LH (I) @ 3AP	0-2
Retinue (ba'irum, sabum kibitum etc.) with axe or sickle-sword, shield and sometimes javelins - Reg Bd (F) @ 6AP	16-42
Retinue archers - Reg Bw (O) @ 5AP	1-4
Sabum qallatum: ½ to ¾ with shield - Reg Ax (O) @ 4AP, remainder without - Reg Ax (I) @ 3AP	4-16
Sabum qallatum with bow or sling - Reg Ps (O) @ 2AP	4-16
Secondary and emergency reserves - Irr Hd (O) @ 1AP	0-12
Nomadic levies with javelins - Irr Ax (I) @ 2AP	0, or 4-18
Nomadic levies with bow or sling - Irr Ps (O) @ 2AP	0, or 2-12
Spies - Irr Ps (I) @ 1AP	0-1
Camp - Reg Bge (O) @ 3AP, or porters or pack-donkeys - Reg Bge (I) @ 2AP	0-2 per general
Ditch and bank perimeter for camp - TF @ 1AP	0, or 1-2 per Bge (O)
Baggage ships - Irr Shp (I) @ 2AP [Bge (O)]	0 or 1 per Bge (O)

Only from 1796 BC to 1776 BC:

Downgrade C-in-C to Inert general (as Iasmah-adad) @ 75AP less	

Only Babylon in 1764 BC:

Mari allies - List: Later Amorite (Bk 1/15)	

Only after 1650 BC:

Replace general's platform car with 2-horse chariot - Reg Cv (S) @ 19AP if ally, 29AP if not	All
Upgrade 2-horse 2-man chariots to Reg Cv (S) @ 9AP	Any

This list covers the armies of the mature, urbanised Amorite dynasties of Syria and Mesopotamia that developed out of the invading Amurru/Early Amorite hordes (covered by list 1/6) before the conquests of the Hittite king Mursilis I opened the way for Hurrian control. They include Yamhad, Karkemish, Qatanum (Qatna), Ebla, and especially the northern kingdom (or so-called Old Assyrian Empire) of Shamshi-Adad and his successors, 1813 BC - 1755 BC, the First Dynasty of Babylon, 1894 BC - 1595 BC (particularly during the reign of Hammurabi, 1792 BC - 1750 BC), Mari until destroyed in 1759 BC and Aleppo until destroyed in 1600 BC.. The early second millennium in the Near East was a time of constantly shifting alliances between the numerous Amorite kingdoms, and large armies often included substantial contingents from allied states.

The new Amorite states basically combined Amorite tactics and equipment with Sumero-Akkadian wealth, culture and technology. The outstanding change from previous civilised armies was the abandonment of standing in close ranks poking at the enemy with long spears in favour of rushing up to him and chopping him with axe or sickle-sword. While effective against infantry, this must have had its weaknesses against chariotry. Sabum qallatum were used in bad going and especially for ambushes. Heavy baggage was usually carried on water transport.

Hurrian immigrants had become a factor after 2200 BC and were the majority of the population around Aleppo, the capital of Yamhad, by 1800 BC. However, they were successfully kept under control by the empires of Akkad and Ur and later the Amorite dynasties, and did not alter the military system. Levies from the powerful semi-nomadic Amorite tribes, in the north and west, such as the Hanu confederation with its Sim'alu ("northerner") and Yaminu ("southerner") branches, or the Sutu, were an important element of armies. Ally-generals' commands need not include nomadic levies. All nomadic levies count as Bedouin.

16. HITTITE OLD AND MIDDLE KINGDOM 1680 BC - 1380 BC

Cool. Ag 3. Rv, DH, SH, GH, Wd, O, V, RF, Rd, BUAf, F.
E: 1/4, 1/15, 1/18, 1/19.

C-in-C: in 2-horse 2-crew chariot - Reg Cv (S) @ 29AP or Reg Cv (O) @ 27AP, or with bow in 2-mule cart - Reg Mtd Bw (O) @ 26AP	1
Sub-general - as above	1-2
2-horse 2-crew chariots - Reg Cv (O) @ 7AP	
- Before 1500 BC:	0-4
- From 1500 BC:	4-9
Scouts - Irr LH (I) @ 3AP	0-1
Standing army spearmen - all Reg Ax (O) @ 4AP or all Reg Pk (F) @ 4AP	16-48
Seasonal army spearmen - Irr Ax (O) @ 3AP	0-72
Archers - Irr Ps (O) @ 2AP or Irr Bw (I) @ 3AP	4-12
Slingers - Irr Ps (O) @ 2AP	4-12
Javelinmen - Irr Ps (I) @ 1AP or Irr Ax (I) @ 2AP	8-24
Hupshu conscripts/levy - Irr Hd (O) @ 1AP	0, or 4-12
Camp - Reg Bge (O) @ 3AP, or pack-donkeys - Reg Bge (I) @ 2AP	0-2 per general

Only in Hattusili's 2nd Syrian campaign sometime between 1630 BC and 1621 BC:

Tikunani allies - List: Later Amorite (Bk 1/15)	

Only from 1620 BC to 1590 BC:

Upgrade C-in-C to Brilliant (as Mursilis I) at 25AP extra	0 or 1

Only Muwa's rebel army in 1400 BC:

Hurrian allies - List: Mitanni (Bk 1/19)	

This list covers the Hittite kingdom from its foundation by the semi-legendary Labarnas possibly circa 1680 BC, until the accession of Suppiluliumas circa 1380 BC. In 1595 BC Mursilis I broke the power of the Amorite states of Syria and overthrew the First Dynasty of Babylon and carried away its gods However, he was murdered before he could consolidate his conquests, leaving power vacuums to be filled by the rising Hurrian powers. The kingdom declined after 1500 BC until it was restored to Empire during the reign of Suppiluliumas from 1380 BC. Records imply that at this time most spearmen had light shields. Some troops remained embodied all year; others were called up during the campaigning season if required. Military officials called "unyanni" ran supply.

17. HYKSOS 1645 BC - 1537 BC

Dry. Ag 2. **WW or Rv,** O, E, V, SF, M, D, Rd, BUAf.
E: 1/2, 1/6, 1/7, 1/15, 1/20, 1/22.

C-in-C in 2-horse 2-crew chariot - Reg Cv (S) @ 29AP	1
Sub-general - as above	0-2
Aamu bedouin ally-general [commanding only Aamu] - Irr Ax (I) @ 7AP	0-2
Retainers with axe or sickle sword and javelins - Reg Bd (F) @ 6AP	16-42
Retainers with bow - Reg Bw (O) @ 5AP	0-4
Light troops with javelins: ½ to ¾ with shield - Reg Ax (O) @ 4AP, remainder without - Reg Ps (I) @ 1AP	4-16
Light troops with bow or sling - Reg Ps (O) @ 2AP	0-12
Aamu bedouin warriors - Irr Ax (I) @ 2AP	0-45
Aamu bedouin or Libyan skirmishers: ½ javelinmen - Irr Ps (I) @ 1AP, ½ with bow or sling - Irr Ps (O) @ 2AP	8-20
Aamu bedouin scouts - up to ½ on horses, remainder on donkeys - Irr LH (I) @ 3AP	0-2
Camp - Irr Bge (O) @ 2AP, or pack-donkeys - Irr Bge (I) @ 1AP	0-2 per general
Egyptian levies - Irr Hd (O) @ 1AP	0-6
Egyptian vassal allies - List: Early Egyptian (Bk 1/2)	
Ahaw - Irr Bts (S) @ 3AP [Any regular foot]	0-2
Only before 1590 BC:	
2-horse, 2-man chariots - Reg Cv (O) @ 7AP	0-3
Only from 1590 BC:	
2-horse, 2-man chariots - Reg Cv (S) @ 9AP	4-12

The Hyksos or "rulers of foreign lands" seized the northern half of Egypt and established a dynasty of rulers that lasted until the 6th, Khamudy, was driven out by Ahmose. An immigration of Aamu nomads into the eastern Delta from 1900 BC had provided a base for a conquest by urban Amorite princes from Syria, pre-eminent amongst who was Sheshy or Salatis. He became Pharaoh, set up a new capital at Avaris and instituted a new religion based on the primacy of the local god Seth. The 400th anniversary of Seth fell in the 34th year of Rameses II, giving a date for the conquest of 1644 BC. This is 50 years before the massed Maryannu chariotry of Mitanni and Canaan, so the theory that chariotry was responsible for the initial Hyksos success is untenable. A core of Later Amorite regulars were based in new fortresses, which garrisons the ruler visited each summer to pay their wages and train them carefully in manoeuvres. Southern Egypt was controlled by doubtfull Egyptian vassals. A new Egyptian dynasty at Thebes rebelled unsuccessfully under Sekenenre (whose mummy shows he died by blows from spears, daggers and axes of Asiatic type, not arrows) and later successfully under Kamose and Ahmose.

18. MINOAN AND EARLY MYCENAEAN 1600 BC - 1250 BC

Warm. Ag 2. S, Rv, DH, SH, GH, O, V, RF, Rd, BUAf, F.
E: 1/16, 1/18, 1/24.

C-in-C - in 2-crew chariot. Reg Kn (F) @ 30AP	1
Sub-general - as above	1-2
Regrade generals in 3-crew or 4-crew chariots to Reg Kn (I) @ 29AP	Any
2-horse 2-crew chariots - Reg Kn (F) @ 10AP or Reg Cv (O) @ 7AP	4-18
Line spearmen - Up to ½ Reg Pk (I) @ 3AP, rest Reg Pk (X) @ 4AP	16-48
Line archers (can support spearmen) - Reg Ps (O) @ 2AP	Up to 1 per 2 Pk elements
Pylians - Reg Ax (I) @ 3AP	0-12
Archers - Irr Ps (O) @ 2AP or Irr Bw (I) @ 3AP	4-12
Slingers - Irr Ps (O) @ 2AP	0-8
Libyans - up to ½ Irr Ps (O) @ 2AP or Irr Bw (I) @ 3AP, rest Irr Ps (I) @ 1AP or Irr Ax (I) @ 2AP	0-15
Camp - Irr Bge (O) @ 2AP, or pack-donkeys - Irr Bge (I) @ 1AP	0-2 per general
Triakonters - Irr Bts (O) @ 2AP [Bd, Pk (X) or Ps]	0-4

This list covers the period of the Aegean Palace Civilization based on the centres of Knossos, Pylos and Mycenae. Charioteers can be mounted knights in Dendra panoply armed with long spear, or lighter warriors in quilted armour with javelins. They either fought en masse in one or two lines in front, or were spaced in groups between spearmen and on their flanks. A very few chariots are depicted with 3 or 4 crew, usually carrying standards. I assume these were not primarily suited for fighting, so grade them as (I) Spearmen typically carried the tower or figure-of-eight shield and held their spears two handed. They fought in close formation, sometimes supported by archers in and/or behind the ranks.

19. MITANNI 1595 BC - 1274 BC

Dry Ag 3. Rv, DH, RH, GH, Wd, O, V, E, SF, Rd, BUAf.
E: 1/4, 1/5, 1/6, 1/15, 1/16, 1/20, 1/21, 1/22, 1/24, 1/25.

C-in-C in 2-horse 2-crew chariot - Reg Cv (S) @ 29AP	1
Sub-general - as above	1-2
Maryannu 2-horse 2-crew chariots - Reg Cv (S) @ 9AP	8-48
Downgrade maryannu 2-horse 2-crew chariots as poorer quality provincials or vassals to Reg Cv (O) @ 7AP	0-15
Mar shipri scouts - Irr LH (I) @ 3AP	0-2
Alik ilki spearmen - Reg Ax (O) @ 4AP	4-15
Alik ilki archers - Reg Ps (O) @ 2AP [can support spearmen], or Reg Bw (I) @ 4AP	4-12
Upgrade alik ilki archers to aweluti qashati or shukituhli - Reg Bw (O) @ 5AP	Up to ¼
Ashshabu levy - Irr Hd (O) @ 1AP	4-16
Hapiru or Akhalamu bedouin skirmishers - up to ½ shielded Irr Ps (S) @ 3AP, remainder Irr Ps (I) @ 1AP	0-8
Camp - Irr Bge (O) @ 2AP, or 2 or 4 wheel wagons - Irr Bge (I) @ 1AP	0-2 per general
Nomad allies - Early Bedouin (Bk 1/6)	

Only before 1340 BC:

Syro-Canaanite allies - List: Syro-Canaanite and Ugaritic (Bk 1)

Only after 1340 BC:

Hittite allies - List: Hittite Empire (Bk 1)

After the fall of the Amorite dynasties and the withdrawal of their Hittite conquerors, Hurrian political control spread out into both Syria and northern Mesopotamia, greatly aided by their recent adoption of massed chariotry techniques possibly acquired from Indo-Iranian contacts. The eastern branch established the Mitannian empire, which comprised several vassal states including Arrapha and Ashur, and provinces such as Hanigalbat, Naharin and the Hurri-lands, and also dominated northern Syria. With its capital at Washshukanni, it was the first superpower in the Middle East.

Its strength lay in its chariot-borne military aristocracy, the maryannu, who served as the archetype of the chariot warrior as a heavily armoured bowman riding in a swift armoured chariot. The army was organised into Left and Right wings. The outlying vassal states and provinces may have provided less well armoured and/or worse drilled maryannu. Aweluti qashati were picked archers sometimes concentrated into separate units and shukituhlu were archers of superior status also carrying a spear and accompanied by an attendant.

20. SYRO-CANAANITE AND UGARITIC 1595 BC - 1100 BC

Warm. Ag 2. S, Rv, GH, Wd, O, V, RF, D, Rd, BUAf, F.
E: 1/4, 1/6, 1/17, 1/19, 1/20, 1/21, 1/22, 1/24, 1/25, 1/27, 1/28, 1/29.

C-in-C in 2-horse 2-crew chariot - Reg Cv (S) @ 29AP	1
Ugaritic sub-general in 2-horse 2-crew chariot - Reg Cv (S) @ 29AP	0-2
Syro-Canaanite or Ugaritic ally-general in 2-horse 2-crew chariot - Reg Cv (S) @ 19AP	1-3
Royal maryannu chariotry - Reg Cv (S) @ 9AP	8-12
Other maryannu chariotry - up to ½ Irr Cv (S) @ 8AP, remainder Irr Cv (O) @ 6AP	12-24
Mounted scouts - Irr LH (I) @ 3AP	0-2
Royal guard - Reg Bw (O) @ 5AP or Reg Bd (F) @ 6AP	0-8
Hupshu, Khepetj or 'Apiru spearmen and javelinmen - up to ½ Irr Ax (O) @ 3AP, remainder Irr Ax (I) @ 2AP or Irr Ps (I) @ 1AP	24-56
Hupshu, Khepetj or 'Apiru archers - Irr Ps (O) @ 2AP or Irr Bw (I) @ 3AP	12-28
Downgrade Hupshu or Khepetj to Irr Hd (O) @ 1AP	0-24
Bedouin (Shaasu or Sutu): up to ½ archers or slingers - Irr Ps (O) @ 2AP, remainder javelinmen - Irr Ax (I) @ 2AP or Irr Ps (I) @ 1AP	0-12
Camp - Irr Bge (O) @ 2AP, or pack-donkeys - Irr Bge (I) @ 1AP	0-2 per general
Only after 1543 BC:	
Egyptian allies - List: New Kingdom Egyptian (Bk 1/22)	
Only before 1340 BC:	
Mitanni allies - List: Mitanni (Bk 1/19)	
Only after 1340 BC:	
Sherden or other Sea Peoples mercenaries - Irr Bd (F) @ 5AP or Irr Bd (O) @ 5AP	0-6
Only if in Ugaritic general's command and after 1340 BC:	
Gasgans - Irr Wb (F) @ 3AP	0-2
Bari - Irr Bts (S) @ 3AP [Ps, Bw, Bd, Ax]	0-8
Marines with fire-pots - Irr Ps (X) @ 6AP	0-1 per 4 Bts
Only if in Ugaritic general's command and after 1275 BC:	
Upgrade Ugaritic royal maryannu chariotry as 3-horse 3-crew to Reg Kn (O) @ 31AP if C-in-C or sub-general, 21AP if ally-general, 11AP if not	Any
Only if in Ugaritic C-in-C's command after 1208 BC:	
Medjergelem guards - Reg Bd (O) @ 7AP	4-6

This list covers the armies of the city-states of Canaan (modern Israel, Palestine and Jordan) and Syria after the fall of some of the Amorite dynasties to the Hittites and occupation of resulting power vacuums by possibly Hurrian rulers commanding chariot-riding maryannu. These city-states were usually now vassals of one of the great powers competing in the area, viz. Mitanni, Egypt, the Hittite Empire and Assyria.

Canaanite tactics relied on the use of high quality maryannu skirmishing chariotry similar to that of Mitanni. Royal maryannu were permanently embodied and centrally equipped and must be in the C-in-C's or an allied command. Other maryannu lived in varying numbers at more distant locations and are assumed to be self-equipped nobles. Captured equipment listed by the Egyptians after Megiddo in 1457 BC suggests about half the maryannu were then armoured. Infantry had a purely subsidiary role. The loose mares in heat used in a vain attempt to disrupt Thutmose III's Egyptian chariots are ignored, since at the very most they would have produced a temporary disorder. Mitanni and Egyptians cannot be used together.

During the Sea Peoples invasion of the Hittite lands and Syria an Ugaritic fleet of 150 ships, carrying an allied Hittite army, destroyed a Sea Peoples fleet off Cyprus. The Hittites then made a fiercely contested landing. Unfortunately, during the fleet's absence, a small Sea People squadron seems to have destroyed Ugarit. Only an Ugaritic C-in-C can have Ugaritic sub-generals. He cannot have an Ugaritic ally-general.

21. KASSITE AND LATER BABYLONIAN 1595 BC - 747 BC

Dry. Ag 1. WW, Rv, GH, O, E, SF, M, Rd, BUAf.
E: 1/4, 1/5, 1/6, 1/12, 1/19, 1/20, 1/24, 1/25, 1/31, 1/42

C-in-C - in chariot, Reg Cv (O) @ 27AP or Reg Cv (S) @ 29AP	1
Sub-general - as above	1-2
Ally-general - in chariot, Reg Cv (O) @ 17AP or Reg Cv (S) @ 19AP	0-2
Chariots - Reg Cv (S) @ 9AP or Reg Cv (O) @ 7AP	8-12
Chariots - Reg Cv (O) @ 7AP	4-12
Mounted scouts - Irr LH (I) @ 3AP	0-2
Militia: ½ spearmen - Irr Ax (O) @ 3AP, ½ archers - Irr Ps (O) @ 2AP [can support other ½]	16-50
Militia archers - Irr Ps (O) @ 2AP or Irr Bw (I) @ 3AP	0-12
Militia slingers - Irr Ps (O) @ 2AP	0-4
Camp - Irr Bge (O) @ 2AP, or pack-donkeys - Irr Bge (I) @ 1AP	0-2 per general
Ditch and bank for camp - TF @ 1AP	0, or 1-2 per Bge (O)
Sutu or Hapiru mercenaries: up to ½ with shield - Irr Ax (O) @ 3AP, remainder without - Irr Ax (I) @ 2AP.	0-24

Only 1124 BC to 1103 BC:

Upgrade C-in-C to Brilliant (as Nebuchadrezzar I) at 25AP extra	0 or 1

Only after 1100 BC:

Early Aramaean allies - List: Early Bedouin (Bk 1/6)	

Only after 890 BC:

Upgrade generals in 3- or 4-horse, 3-crew chariots to Reg Kn (O) @ 31AP if C-in-C or sub-general, 21AP if	
ally-general	All
Upgrade Cv (S) chariots to 3- or 4- horse 3-crew, Reg Kn (O) @ 11AP	0-6
Cavalry - Reg Cv (I) @ 6AP	1-4
Arab allies - List: Early Bedouin (Bk 1/6)	0-24

Only from 851 BC to 824 BC:

Assyrian allies - List: Middle Assyrian and Early Neo-Assyrian (Bk 1/25)	

This list covers the Babylonian empire in Mesopotamia from the Kassite (3rd) dynasty's first occupation of the throne of Babylon until its overthrow by the Elamites in 1157 BC, the succeeding 2nd Dynasty of Isin (4th), the anarchy following the Aramaean invasions, then a period under weak and often foreign-influenced later dynasties, prior to the accession in 746 BC of Nabu-nasir.

The Kassites arrived in Babylonia from Iran as the old Babylonian kingdom (List 15 Later Amorite) fell into decline. After the Hittites under Mursilis I sacked Babylon, a Kassite dynasty took over control. At this time southern Babylonia was the independent country of "Sealand" (List 12 Sumerian Successor States), but this was reconquered by 1460 and Karduniash (as Kassite Babylon was called) became recognised as a major power. Its military campaigns were mainly against Sutu nomads, the Elamites and Assyria. It was weakened by an unsuccessful invasion of Assyria under Kashtiliash I (1242 BC - 1235 BC) and the dynasty fell when Babylon was sacked by the Elamites in 1157 BC.

Babylon regained its position under the 2nd Dynasty of Isin when Nebuchadrezzar I (1126 BC - 1105 BC) won a major victory over the Elamites and recaptured the sacred statue of Marduk that the Elamites had carried off after the sack, but though clever, energetic and a master of surprise he was apt to overreach himself and fared less well against the Assyrians.

Succeeding dynasties were unable to prevent large scale immigration by Aramaean tribes and had to come to terms with this. A recently discovered letter from an Aramaean chieftain to the Babylonians says in effect "Great, so we're now allies. Who do we attack?"

22. NEW KINGDOM EGYPTIAN 1543 BC - 1069 BC

Dry. Ag 2. O. E, Rd, BUAf. In Delta: **Rv,** M, otherwise **WW**, RF.
E: 1/3, 1/6, 1/7, 1/17, 1/19, 1/20, 1/24, 1/27, 1/28, 1/29, 1/31.

C-in-C in 2-horse 2-crew chariot - Reg Cv (S) @ 29AP	1
Sub-general - as above	2-3
2-horse 2-crew chariots - Reg Cv (S) @ 9AP	8-24
Scouts riding horse in donkey style - Irr LH (I) @ 3AP	0-1
Egyptian Royal Guard with textile armour and short heavy spear - Reg Bd (F) @ 6AP	0-2
Egyptian close fighters with spear, light shield and side arm - Reg Ax (O) @ 4AP or Reg Bd (I) @ 5AP	8-32
Upgrade Egyptian close fighters to men with heavy weighted axe - Reg Bd (X) @ 8AP	0-4
Egyptian archers - Reg Bw (I) @ 4AP	8-32
Egyptian light archers - Reg Ps (O) @ 2AP	0-8
Downgrade Egyptian regular infantry to "undisciplined": Reg Ax (O to Irr Ax (O) @4AP, Bd (I) to Irr Bd (I) @ 4AP, Bd (X) to Irr Bd (X) @ 6AP, Bw (I) to Irr BW (I) @ 3AP, Ps (O) to Irr (Ps (O) @ 2AP	All or none
Syro-Canaanite javelinmen -up to ½ shielded Irr Ax (O) @ 3AP, remainder Irr Ax (I) @ 2AP or Irr Ps (I) @ 1AP	0-6
Nubian or Syro-Canaanite archers - Irr Ps (O) @ 2AP	0-8
Libyan, Palestinian or Bedouin javelinmen - Irr Ps (I) @ 1AP	0-8
Camp - Reg Bge (O) @ 3AP, or ox-carts, pack-donkeys, women and camp followers - Reg Bge (I) @ 2AP	0-2 per general
Camp defences of ditch, bank and shields - TF @ 1AP	1-2 per Bge (O)
Bari - Irr Bts (S) @ 3AP [Bw, Bd, Ps]	0-4
Only from 1457 BC to 1429 BC:	
Upgrade C-in-C to Brilliant (as Thutmose III) at 25AP extra	0 or 1
Only from 1450 BC to 1176 BC:	
Syro-Canaanite maryannu in 2-horse 2-crew chariots - up to ½ Reg Cv (S) @ 9AP, remainder - Irr Cv (O) @ 6AP	0-4
Gasgan mercenaries/slave soldiers - Irr Wb (F) @ 3AP	0-4
Only until 1279 BC:	
Aegean mercenaries - Reg Ax (I) @ 3AP	0-2
Only 1279 BC to 1213 BC:	
Downgrade C-in-C to Inert general (as Rameses II) @ 75AP less	0 or 1
Only from 1276 BC:	
Shardana Royal Guard - Reg Bd (O) @ 7AP	0-2
Only after 1200 BC:	
Upgrade Reg Ax (O) to Reg Bd (F) @ 6AP and Reg Bd (I) to Reg Bd (O) @ 7AP	All
Libyan swordsmen - Irr Wb (F) @ 3AP	8-16
Sherden - Irr Bd (O) @ 5AP or Irr Bd (F) @ 5AP	4-16
Only from 1175 BC to 1143 BC:	
Sea Peoples military colonists - Irr Bd (F) @ 5AP	8-20

This list starts with Kamose's revolt against the Hyksos and ends with the death of Rameses XI, at the end of whose reign Nubia had been lost, the remainder of the south had come under the control of the High Priests of Amun at Thebes, and the north was disputed by Libyan-influenced petty kings. New Kingdom Egyptian armies added massed chariotry to the already sophisticated infantry tactics of the Middle Kingdom, but continued to rely heavily on their infantry, although both Thutmose III at Megiddo and Rameses II at Kadesh berate these for indiscipline, hence rhe irregular alternative. In the hands of competent generals chariotry supported and protected the infantry rather than vice versa. This difference probably resulted from the different structure of society as well as Egypt's greater population and hence greater reserves of manpower. The army was permanently organised into 3 or 4 mixed corps and at Kadesh these seem to have moved separately. Accordingly, if a 3rd sub-general is used, each general must have at least ¼ of the minima of each compulsory regular troop type.

When fighting enemy chariots, particularly the shock chariots of the Hittites, Egyptian chariots aimed to cause maximum casualties from arrows and javelins while avoiding close contact. Chariot runners are not represented separately, but suitable figures can be added to the chariots' bases for appearance. Early New Kingdom close fighters are often depicted running with axe in right hand, spear in left, and smallish shield slung behind shoulder. In other pictures they are shown advancing at the walk with overlapping shields, although still carrying their spear in the left hand. Later New Kingdom close fighters have bigger shields, wear body armour, and are sometimes depicted thrusting 2-handed with their spears. The heavy weighted axe users are usually depicted mixed with other axemen By 1200 BC, substantial numbers of Libyan and Sherden mercenaries were supplanting native troops and after the defeat of the Sea Peoples in 1176 BC, very large numbers of these were incorporated into the army to man garrisons both within Egypt and to the north.

The most famous (and over-rated) Egyptian general of this period is Rameses II (1279-1213), who concealed his sub-standard performance at Kadesh in 1274 BC by spin-doctoring his monuments and blaming subordinates in true wargamer style. Rameses III (1184-1153), who beat the dangerous invasions of a Libyan confederacy in the 5th year of his reign (1179) and the Sea Peoples in his 8th year (1176), makes a better role model; and Thutmose III (1479-1425), by far the greatest Egyptian commander, a better one yet.   WW represents the Nile, Rv the branches of its delta.

23. VEDIC INDIAN 1500 BC - 512 BC

Tropical. Ag 2. Rv, GH, **Wd**, E, SF, M, Rd, BUAf.
E: 1/5, 1/10, 1/23, 1/25, 1/43, 1/60,

C-in-C - in chariot, Irr Cv (S) @ 18AP	1
Sub-general - as above	0-1
Indian ally-general in chariot - Irr Cv (S) @ 13AP	1-2
Heroic charioteers - Irr Cv (S) @ 8AP	12-27
Cavalry - Irr Cv (I) @ 5AP	0-8
Bodyguard swordsmen - Irr Bd (F) @ 5AP	0-1
Archers - Irr Bw (I) @ 3AP	24-72
Mountaineers with slings - Irr Ps (O) @ 2AP	0-4
Followers - Irr Hd (O) @ 1AP	
- until 1100 BC:	0-15
- after 1100 BC:	0-6
Camp - Irr Bge (O) @ 2AP, or pack-donkeys or ox-wagons - Irr Bge (I) @ 1AP	0-2 per general
Only after 900 BC:	
Upgrade sub-general to Irr El (S) @ 30AP	0-1
Upgrade generals still in chariots to Irr Kn (I) @ 17AP if C-in-C or sub-general, 12AP if ally-general	All/0
Elephants - Irr El (S) @ 20AP	0-2

This list covers Indian armies from the Aryan invasion of India from the north until the Persian conquest of the north-west and the establishment of the first Buddhist states. The main sources are the Vedas and the Mahabharata. Chariotry was the favoured arm and mount of generals, although lesser generals are sometimes described as temporarily fighting from elephant back. Generals in chariots can always dismount, either as Bowmen (S) or with the favourite heavy club as Blades (X).

Most chariots had two unarmoured horses and were crewed by an armoured noble archer and his driver. Generals later had heavier chariots with a parasol, often drawn by 4 horses, sometimes armoured, and with a crew of up to 4. However, the extra 2 men do not appear in accounts of combat and may have been accompanying on foot as "wheel guards". If this interpretation is chosen, the chariot is still classed as Cv (S), despite its 4 horses. If not, classification as irregular Kn has the incidental effect of encouraging the heroic behaviour that dominates the Indian epics. Modern replica 4 horse chariots in epic films seem to be remarkably clumsy.

Javelin cavalry supported the chariots on the flanks, fairly ineffectively. Elephants appear first in groups protecting the join of the army's centre to its wings, each manned by up to 12 men, of which 8 probably fought on foot. Foot were mainly archers clumped in masses to the rear and incapable of resisting hand to hand. Spears were predominantly mounted weapons. There is one reference to bodyguard swordsmen dressed in red. The higher number of hordes in the early period represents the poorer migrants.

24. HITTITE EMPIRE 1380 BC - 1170 BC

Cool. Ag 2. Rv, DH, SH, GH, Wd, O, V, RF, Rd, BUAf, F.
E: 1/4, 1/6, 1/18, 1/19, 1/20, 1/21, 1/22, 1/24, 1/25, 1/26, 1/28.

C-in-C in 2-horse 2-crew chariot - Reg Cv (S) @ 29AP	1
Sub-general - as above	0-2
Hittite and allied 2-horse 2-crew chariots - Reg Cv (S) @ 9AP	4-16
Hittite scouts - Reg LH (F) @ 5AP	0-3
Hittite standing army or seasonal army spearmen - Reg Pk (F) @ 4AP	8-36
Hittite conscripts - Irr Hd (O) @ 1AP	0-20
Camp - Reg Bge (O) @ 3AP, or pack-donkeys or ox-wagons - Reg Bge (I) @ 2AP	0-2 per Reg general
Anatolian vassal ally-general in 2-horse 2-crew chariot commanding only Anatolian vassals - Irr Cv (O) @ 11 AP	0-2
Anatolian vassal or Gasgan 2-horse 2-crew chariots - Irr Cv (O) @ 6AP	4-9
Anatolian vassal spearmen - Irr Ax (O) @ 3AP	4-12
Anatolian vassal and Gasgan archers and slingers - Irr Ps (O) @ 2AP	0-9
Gasgan warriors - Irr Wb (F) @ 3AP	0-12
Lukka - Irr Bd (F) @ 5AP	0-4
Camp - Irr Bge (O) @ 2AP, or pack-donkeys or ox-wagons - Irr Bge (I) @ 1AP	0-2 per Irr general
Only from 1380 BC to 1335 BC:	
Upgrade C-in-C to Brilliant (as Suppiliumas) at 25AP extra	0 or 1
Only after 1348 BC:	
Mitanni allies - List: Hurri-Mitanni (Bk 1/19)	
Only after 1340 BC:	
Syrian vassal ally-general in 2-horse 2-crew chariot [commanding only Syrians or Bedouin] - Reg Cv (S) @ 19AP	0-2
Syro-Canaanite vassal 2-horse 2-crew chariots - up to ½ Reg Cv (S) @ 9AP, remainder - Irr Cv (O) @ 6AP	*4-12
Syrian vassal scouts - Irr LH (I) @ 3AP	0-1 per Syrian ally general
Syrian vassal guards - Reg Bw (O) @ 5AP or Reg Bd (F) @ 6AP	0-4
Syrian vassal spearmen and javelinmen - up to ½ Irr Ax (O) @ 3AP, remainder Irr Ax (I) @ 2AP or Irr Ps (I) @ 1AP	*8-24
Syrian vassal archers - Irr Ps (O) @ 2AP or Irr Bw (I) @ 3AP	*4-12
Downgrade Syrian foot to Irr Hd (O) @ 1AP	0-20
Bedouin (Shaasu or Sutu): up to ½ archers or slingers - Irr Ps (O) @ 2AP, remainder javelinmen - Irr Ax (O) @ 3AP or Irr Ax (I) @ 2AP or Irr Ps (I) @ 1AP	0-12
Ugaritic bari - Irr Bts (S) @ 3AP [any foot]	0-8
Ugaritic marines with fire pots - Irr Ps (X) @ 6AP	0-1 per 4 Bts
Only after 1208 BC:	
Upgrade vassal Syrian guards as Ugaritic to Reg Bd (O) @ 7AP	0-2
Only after 1275 BC:	
Upgrade Hittite and allied Reg Cv (S) chariots to 3-crew Reg Kn (O) @ 31AP if general, 11AP if not	All
Upgrade Syrian regular chariots to 3-crew as Ugaritic - Reg Kn (O) @ 21AP if ally-general, Reg Kn (O) @ 11AP if not	0-4
Only in 1274 BC:	
Upgrade C-in-C to Brilliant (as Muwatallis) at 25AP extra	0 or 1

This list covers the Hittite empire of eastern Asia Minor from the accession of Suppiliumas circa 1380 BC. Mitanni was acquired as a vassal state circa 1348 BC. Syria (including allied or feudatory states such as the Canaanites, Phoenicians, Retennu, Ugaritics and Khaaru) was incorporated into the empire circa 1340 BC. The empire was crippled by the "Sea Peoples" invasion of the 1170s and then finished off by their old Gasgan enemies. At the battle of Kadesh in 1274 BC, Hittite chariots and those of their allies from Arzawa, Masa and Pitassa had three-man crews, comprising shieldless driver, shieldless spearman (who probably also had a bow) and shield-bearer. Against lighter chariots these would attempt to come to close quarters where their long spears and larger crew would have the advantage. Since they apparently came as a surprise to the Egyptians, they were probably a recent innovation. A Hittite army would still include 2-man chariot types, including Syrian chariots with driver and archer, and Anatolian types with driver and a single spearmen or javelinman.

The duties of Hittite scouts included eliminating enemy scouts, so they are classed as (F) instead of the more usual (I).

Infantry at Kadesh are depicted deployed in the rear in deep rectangular blocks of tight-packed troops with spear in one hand and sword in the other, and are described in the Egyptian account of the battle as "teheru", a term they also used for their own elite troops. Only officers are shown with shields. Spears are elsewhere often shown as long and used two-handed. In Anatolia, the Hittite infantry were well suited to counter the troublesome Gasgans in rugged terrain.

Anatolian, Syrian or Ugaritic vassal troops must be commanded by a vassal ally-general of their own nation if such is present, otherwise by any Hittite general. Minima marked * apply only if any Syrians, Ugaritics or Bedouin are used. An Ugaritic fleet landed a Hittite force to attack Cyprus.

25. MIDDLE ASSYRIAN AND EARLY NEO-ASSYRIAN 1365 BC - 745 BC

Dry. Ag 4. WW, Rv, DH, RH, GH, Wd, O, E, SF, Rd, BUAf.
E: 1/4, 1/5, 1/6, 1/19, 1/20, 1/21, 1/23, 1/24, 1/31, 1/34, 1/35, 1/37, 1/38, 1/39, 1/40, 1/41, 1/42.

C-in-C: in 2-crew chariot - Reg Cv (S) @ 29AP, in side-saddle horse litter - Reg Cv (I) @ 26AP, or on	
foot - Reg Bw (O) @ 25AP	1
Sub-general in 2-crew chariot - Reg Cv (S) @ 29AP	1-2
Sha shepe and palace chariots with 2 horses, 2 crew - Reg Cv (S) @ 9AP	8-18
Mounted scouts - Irr LH (I) @ 3AP	0-2
Ashsharittu or huradu (elite troops) - ½ Reg Bd (F) @ 6AP, ½ Reg Ps (O) @ 2AP [can support other ½]	8-24
Hupshu or sabe (peasant militia) - ½ Irr Ax (O) @ 3AP, ½ Irr Ps (O) @ 2AP [can support other ½]	0-48
Levy archers - Irr Ps (O) @ 2AP or Irr Bw (I) @ 3AP	0-24
Siege machines - Reg WWg (S) @ 14AP	0-3
Camp - Irr Bge (O) @ 2AP, or pack-animals or ox-carts - Irr Bge (I) @ 1AP	0-2 per general
Rafts of inflated goatskin - Irr Bts (I) @ 1AP [Any foot]	0-6
Only 1274 BC to 1245 BC:	
Upgrade C-in-C to Brilliant (as Shalmaneser I or Tukulti-Ninurta) at 25AP extra	0 or 1
Only 1115 BC to 1077 BC:	
Upgrade C-in-C to Brilliant (as Tiglath-Pileser I) at 25AP extra	0 or 1
Only after 1115 BC:	
Gamarriia or kallapani (vehicle mounted infantry) - ½ Reg Mtd Bd (F) @ 8AP, ½ Reg Mtd Ps (O) @ 3 AP [can support other ½]	0-2
Only after 890 BC:	
Neo-Hittite and Aramaean allies - List: Neo-Hittite and Later Aramaean (Bk 1/31)	
Only from 890 BC to 860 BC:	
Pethalle (cavalry teams of archer and companion) - all Irr Cv (I) @ 5AP or all LH (I) @ 3AP	2-4
Only 883 BC to 859 BC:	
Upgrade C-in-C to Brilliant (as Ashurnasirpal II) at 25AP extra	0 or 1
Only from 883 BC:	
Upgrade generals' chariots to 3-horse 3-crew - Reg Kn (O) @ 31AP	All
Upgrade chariots to 3-horse 3-crew - Reg Kn (O) @ 11AP	Up to ½
Mud-brick and timber defences for camp - TF @ 1AP	0, or 1-2 per Bge (O)

Only after 860 BC:

Pethalle (cavalry teams of archer and companion) - Irr Cv (I) @ 5AP	4-6
Subject, second-rate or unwilling levies - Irr Hd (O) @ 1AP	5-10

Only after 825 BC:

Ally-general in 3- or 4-horse 3-crew chariot - Reg Kn (O) @ 21AP	0-2

Only Regency of Sammuramat from 810 BC to 806 BC:

Replace Cv (S) chariots with camels disguised as elephants - Irr Cm (X) @ 7AP	0-3

Only 772 BC to 745 BC:

Downgrade C-in-C to Inert general (as Ashur-dan III or Ashur-nirari) @ 75AP less	0 or 1

This list covers the seasonal, pre-reform army of Assyria in which Hurri-Mitannian practice was the strongest influence. At this date the Assyrian army was probably organised into no more than two corps, or wings. If the C-in-C represents the turtanu rather than the king or regent, then only the minimum permitted ashsharittu and huradu are allowed. The instability of Assyria from the latter part of Shalmaneser III's reign until the reign of Tiglath-Pileser III is represented by the conditions post 825 BC. Chariots can be dismounted as Bw (X) instead of Bw (O) to attack fortifications. Pethalle teams are graded as irregular because of the difficulty in manoeuvring pairs of cavalrymen of whom one rider leads the other's horse. Pethalle elements should be of 2 instead of the normal 3 cavalry figures, with the archer on the right and the companion leading his mount on his left. Hupshu are assumed to include vassal as well as native contingents. Each element of supporting Ps (O) must initially deploy with the element it nominally supports. Gamarriia/Kallapani were infantry carried on fast flat-bed carts, like those of the Elamites. Dummy elephants are dubiously stated by Ktesias to have been used against an Indian army by Queen Semiramis, who is equated with Sammuramat, Queen-regent of Assyria between 810 - 806 BC. His source may have been a garbled account of Assyrian siege machines as shown on page 200 of AANE. Shalmaneser III used rafts to fight a bloody battle against reed boats on the Caspian in 846 BC. Siege machines can only be deployed if the enemy has PF. Camp fortifications are first attested under Ashurnasirpal II after 884 BC. They were not constructed after each march but established as a local base for the area of operations. Several Assyrian kings of this period used swift movement over unlikely terrain to surprise their enemies, not always with full success. Ashur-dan III (772 BC - 755 BC) and Ashu-nirari V (754 BC - 745 BC) were weak kings dominated by officials, especially the prominent elderly general Shamshi-ilu, and campaigned themselves only rarely and ineffectively.

26. LATER MYCENAEAN AND TROJAN WAR 1250 BC - 1190 BC

Warm. Ag 1 if Trojan, 3 if not. S, Rv, DH, SH, GH, O, V, RF, Rd, BUAf, F. Trojan: **BUAf** if no Hittites used.
E: 1/14, 1/24, 1/26, 1/28.

C-in-C - in chariot, Irr Cv (O) @ 16AP	1
Sub-general - as above	1-2
Heroic charioteers - Irr Cv (O) @ 6AP	12-24
Cavalry - Irr Cv (I) @ 5AP	0-4
Spearmen - Irr Sp (I) @ 3AP	24-75
Javelinmen - Irr Ps (I) @ 1AP	4-18
Archers - Irr Ps (O) @ 2AP or Irr Bw (I) @ 3AP	4-12
Slingers - Irr Ps (O) @ 2AP	0-8
Camp - Irr Bge (O) @ 2AP, or slaves or ox-wagons - Irr Bge (I) @ 1AP	0-2 per general

Only Achaians:

Achaian ally-general (Achilles) in chariot - Irr Cv (O) @ 11AP	*1
Upgrade Achilles to Brilliant general @ 25 AP extra	0 or 1
Achilles' Myrmidons - all Irr Wb (S) @ 5AP or all Irr Bd (O) @ 5AP	*4-6
Upgrade C-in-C and sub-generals to Reg Cv (O) @ 27AP, heroic charioteers other than those of Achilles to Reg Cv (O) @ 7AP, spearmen to Reg Sp (I) @ 4AP and archers to Reg Ps (O) @ 2AP or Reg Bw (I) @ 4AP	All/0

Pylian sub-general in chariot (Nestor) commanding all and only Pylians - Reg Kn (F) @ 30AP	*1
Pylian charioteers - Reg Kn (F) @ 10AP	*4-6
Pylian spearmen - up to ½ Reg Pk (I) @ 3AP, remainder Reg Pk (X) @ 4AP	*8-12
Pylian archers - Reg Ps (O) @ 2AP [can support Pylian spearmen]	0-6
Wooden horse - Irr WWg (S) @ 10AP	0-1
Triakonters - Irr Bts (O) @ 2AP [Any foot]	0-4
Horse transports - Irr Shp (I) @ 2AP [Chariots]	0-1
Ditch and bank for camp - TF @ 1AP	0-16

Only Trojans:

Sarpedon's Lukka warriors - Irr Bd (F) @ 5AP	*4-8
Early Thracians (Thrakes, Kikones) - Irr Ps (S) @ 3AP	4-12
Hittite allies - List: Hittite Empire (Bk 1/24)	0-24

This list covers the later period of Mycenaean Greece and the semi-legendary Trojan War of about 1200 BC (possibly 1193 BC to 1183 BC) described in Homer's "Iliad", which is now thought to be a heavily embroidered account of an actual conflict between Achaian Greeks and the similar culture of Troy/Ilium/Ilion on the west coast of Asia Minor that controlled access to the Black Sea; and to reflect the military practises of this era or sometimes of that following.

The option to upgrade Achaians to regular is in case the military structure of the Palace Culture was still in place. The elderly and conservative Nestor's Pylians are represented as using the tactics of the earlier period. Other spearmen are described by Homer as pressing "shield against shield" and "in their closed formation, dark as a cloud, bristling with shields and spears". Outside Homer, the Warrior Vase infantry have each a single spear and no sword. Achilles is represented as an irregular ally-general of the same nation to give a chance of unreliability, but not of changing sides. His chariots are assumed to have been as ill-disciplined as the rest of his contingent. He must command all Myrmidons and cannot command any other foot or any regular charioteers. Myrmidons were noted for "thrift, patience and tenacity" but also for intemperate pillage and atrocity. Achilles is given the option to be brilliant as a flawed [possibly psychotic] hero. Nestor must command all Pylians. Generals and charioteers can always dismount as Bd (O). Minima marked * apply only if any troops of that commander are used. One explanation of the wooden horse is as an Assyrian-type siege tower. It can be deployed only if the enemy has PF. Sufficient shipping is provided for a raiding party such as that of Achilles. Although classed as ships, horse transports are ordinary triakonters carrying horses and dismantled chariots instead of foot, so with few rowers.

Troy/Ilium/Ilion is taken to be the Wilusa of Hittite records. This was within the Hittite sphere of influence and a Hittite army was sent to aid it against Attarsiyas (Atreus?), a ruler of the Ahhiyawa (Achaians?) at some time during the reign of the Hittite king Tudhaliya IV (1250 BC to 1220 BC). A Hittite allied contingent cannot include Syrians, Ugaritics, Gasgans or Bedouins. Amazon allies appear in Homer only when the old king Priam is said to have fought against them in his youth and in later interpolations. This is more than 500 years too early for horse archers, but there are many Greek depictions of Amazons fighting on foot with bow and light axe to excuse having an element or so among Trojan Ps (O).

The Trojan war can be seen as a precursor to the Sea Peoples invasions that brought down several major near eastern states shortly afterwards. Once one major power had fallen to an attack from the sea, raids and afterwards larger attacks were encouraged by the prospect of large profits and perceptions of potential victim weakness. Indeed, participants from both sides in the war can be plausibly identified among the later invaders.

As you might expect from its inclusion of Trojan pack-llamas, the film "Troy" is not a good guide.

27. EARLY HEBREW c. 1250 BC - 1000 BC

Warm. Ag 3. L, Rv, **DH**, SH, RH, GH, Wd, O, V, RF, G, Rd, BUA, F.
E: 1/6, 1/20, 1/22, 1/29, 1/31.

C-in-C - Irr Ax (S) @ 14AP	1
Sub-general - as above, or Irr Ps (S) @ 13AP	1-2
Ark of the Covenant guarded by Levites - Irr Bge (S) @ 3AP	0-1
Simeonites - Irr Wb (F) @ 3AP	0-12
Ephraimites - Irr Wb (F) @ 3AP	0-12
Benjaminite archers - Irr Ps (O) @ 2AP or Irr Bw (I) @ 3AP	0-12
Benjaminite slingers - Irr Ps (O) @ 2AP	0-15
Gadite skirmishers - Irr Ps (S) @ 3AP	0-15
Issacharian scouts - Irr Ps (I) @ 1AP	0-15
Other tribesmen - Irr Ax (O) @ 3AP	40-120
Camp - Irr Bge (O) @ 2AP, or pack-donkeys - Irr Bge (I) @ 1AP	0-2 per general

Only if C-in-C is Joshua from c. 1210 BC to 1200 BC	
Upgrade C-in-C to Brilliant general @ 25AP extra.	0 or 1
Gibeonite vassals - Irr Hd (O) @ 1AP	0-6

Only if C-in-C is Gideon from c. 1130 BC to 1120 BC:	
Upgrade C-in-C to Brilliant general @ 25AP extra.	0 or 1
Upgrade "other tribesmen" to picked men - Irr Ax (S) @ 4AP	1-2
Ally-general of same nation commanding all and only Ephraimites - Irr Wb (F) @ 8AP	0 or 1

Only if C-in-C is Saul from c. 1020 BC:	
Retained mercenaries - Irr Ax (S) @ 4AP	0-15
Ditch and bank for camp - TF @ 1AP	0, or 1-2 per Bge (O)

This list covers Hebrew armies from the selection of Joshua as Judge until David's accession, and is largely based on the Bible; which is unreliable history but the best available. The dates used here are those most usually quoted. Simeonites and Ephraimites are referred to as "mighty men of valour", Gadites as accustomed to spear and target and "swift as roes upon the mountain", Issachar as expert scouts, and several other tribes as armed with spear and shield or with a mixture of weapons suitable for close combat. Benjaminites are not only expert with bow and sling but ambidextrous. Lacking chariots, Hebrew armies of this period dealt with their exponents by striking first, usually with flank charges from difficult terrain. Joshua and Gideon were both masters of surprise and mobility, using night marches and expert scouts. As Proverbs 20, 18 says "With ruses make war". A 3rd century AD synagogue painting shows the Ark of the Covenant as a vertical dome-topped chest, golden brown in colour and decorated with bands and iron fittings, on a similar coloured plinth carried shoulder high on litter poles by 4 men and escorted by swordsmen. It has also been recently reinterpreted as a massive portable drum, the noise of which demoralised opponents. The Canaanite townsmen of Gibeon submitted to Joshua and fought reluctantly on his side, but after being found to have deceived the Hebrews were temporarily reduced to "hewers of wood and drawers of water". Gideon's 300 picked men can be distinguished by giving some trumpets or large jars in addition to weapons. The trumpets will look well in sieges as well as in night attacks! Ephraimites fought under Gideon as an independent contingent. Gideon cannot command Simeonites, Benjaminites, Gadites or Issacharians, or be accompanied by the Ark. Camp defences are first mentioned under Saul, who also recruited renowned warriors of many origins to his following.

28. SEA PEOPLES 1208 BC - 1176 BC

Warm. Ag 4. <u>S</u>, Rv, GH, RF. D, Rd.
E: 1/4, 1/7, 1/20, 1/22, 1/24, 1/26.

C-in-C - in chariot Irr Cv (O) @ 16AP, or on foot, Irr Bd (O) @ 15AP	1
Sub-general - as above	1-3
Chariots with driver and 2 javelinmen - Irr Cv (O) @ 6AP	0-6
Chieftains and their retinues, armoured, with sword and/or spear and shield - Irr Bd (O) @ 5AP	0-20
Common warriors of most Sea People nations, with pairs of javelins, shield and sword - Irr Bd (F) @ 5AP	32-66
Sheklesh or Teresh: shieldless javelinmen - Irr Ax (I) @ 2AP or Irr Ps (I) @ 1AP	8-24
Migrant families - Irr Hd (O) @ 1AP	0-12
Bird-headed boats - Irr Bts (O) @ 2AP [Bd (O)]	0-7
Camp - Irr Bge (O) @ 2AP, or ox-carts - Irr Bge (I) @ 1AP	0-2 per general
Ox-carts manned by warriors - Irr WWg (I) @ 4AP	0-1 per 2 Bge (I)
Ox-cart laager to protect camp - TF @ 1AP	0, or 1-2 per Bge (O)

During the 12th century BC, Anatolia, Egypt, Canaan and Syria came under increasing pressure from raids by the so-called "Sea Peoples", the success of which encouraged larger scale invasions. Previous employment as mercenaries may have increasingly convinced them that the old Bronze Age cities were a lucrative and vulnerable target. Who they were is uncertain, but it is no longer thought that all came from Anatolia. The Sherden probably came from Sardinia, the Lukka from Lykia, Peleset from Crete, and Sheklesh possibly from Sicily. The Ekwesh may have been Achaians. The Denyen and Tjekker dressed like Peleset so may be related. Teresh probably came from northern Syria. The Weshwesh are currently unclaimed. The command system specified here assumes a single dominant (unknown) leader whose prestige attracted participants from far afield.

The Hittite Empire collapsed under the onslaught. Ugarit was destroyed sometime between 1196 BC and 1179 BC. Egypt repulsed an assault by Libyans with massive Sea Peoples assistance in 1179 BC, but a second invasion from Syria in 1176 BC was only repulsed by an extreme national effort. Thereafter the confederacy appears to have dispersed to their homelands, or settled in Syria, where most were quickly absorbed by the local culture. The Peleset gave their name to Palestine and became the Philistines.

It has recently been suggested that the Sea People's success and the fall of the chariot powers was not due to overwhelming numbers of a mass migration, but to military innovation - infantry with a long sword, a pair of javelins and often body armour being able to both resist the charge of chariots and to easily sweep away the poor quality foot supporting these. The Sea Peoples themselves used a lesser but still considerable number of chariots with 2 javelinmen and possibly a bow. These can always dismount as Bd (O). Their foot are described by the Egyptians as "teheru", meaning elite close combat infantry. These are depicted as running but fighting in a shallow line. Egyptian reliefs show Sea Peoples' ships as probably identical to later Helladic triakonters. Though no one is depicted rowing, this is probably because the rowers were also the fighting crew, so are otherwise occupied. The crews are all depicted armoured. The ox-carts shown in one battle scene partially manned by warriors, but mostly occupied by families, are mobile baggage, possibly supplemented with looted flocks and herds. Alternatively, they can be used as a wagon laager to protect baggage and families. This is not however attested by the Egyptian reliefs, possibly because the horde was caught on the march.

29. PHILISTINE 1166 BC - 600 BC

Warm. Ag 3. S, Rv, GH, RF, O, V, D, Rd, BUAf, F.
E: 1/6, 1/20, 1/22, 1/27, 1/29, 1/31, 1/34, 1/35, 1/38, 1/45, 1/51, 1/53.

C-in-C in chariot as below - Irr Cv (O) @ 16AP or Irr Bd (O) @ 15AP	1
Philistine sub-general - as above	1-2
Chariots with driver and 2 javelinmen - Irr Cv (O) @ 6AP	7-20
Mounted scouts - Irr LH (I) @ 3AP	0-2
Elite swordsmen - Irr Bd (O) @ 5AP	0-6
Swordsmen - Irr Bd (F) @ 5AP	24-39
Javelinmen - Up to ½ Irr Ax (O) @ 3AP, remainder Irr Ax (I) @ 2AP or Irr Ps (I) @ 1AP	12-40
Archers - Irr Ps (O) @ 2AP or Irr Bw (I) @ 3AP	0-10
Slingers - Irr Ps (O) @ 2AP	0-5
Kharu archers - Irr Ps (O) @ 2AP or Irr Bw (O) @ 4AP	0-4
Camp - Irr Bge (O) @ 2AP, or pack-donkeys or ox-wagons - Irr Bge (I) @ 1AP	0-2 per general
Canaanite allies - List: Syro-Canaanite and Ugaritic (Bk 1/20)	

Only after 1100 BC:

Upgrade chariots to Reg Cv (S) with driver and archer @ 29AP if general, otherwise 9AP	All
Regrade general on foot and elite swordsmen as elite spearmen - Reg Sp (O) @ 25AP if general, 5AP if not	All
Regrade swordsmen as spearmen - Reg Sp (I) @ 4AP	All
Phoenician allies - List: Cypriot and Phoenician (Bk 1/35)	
Aramaean allies - List: Neo-Hittite and Later Aramaean (Bk 1/31)	

Only from 1025 BC to 1020 BC:

Add Goliath of Gath and followers as Irr Bd (X) @ 6AP, or as Brilliant sub-general - Irr Bd (X) @ 41AP	0 or 1
Only from 1006 BC to 1003 BC:	
Hebrew mercenary Gibborim - Irr Ax (S) @ 4AP	0-4

Only from 734 BC to 720 BC:

Egyptian allies - List: Libyan Egyptian (Bk 1/38)

Only in 701 BC:

Egyptian allies - List: Kushite Egyptian (Bk 1/46)

The Philistines, whose name derives from the Peleset, were descended from Sea Peoples settled in Palestine by Rameses III as military colonists after the defeat of their invasion. Within 10 years, they had regained much autonomy and by around 1140 BC they had cast off Egyptian control and were expanding both northwards along the coast and south into Egyptian territory. Their five cities - Ashdod, Askelon, Ekron, Gath and Gaza - were each ruled by a prince, but they usually acted in consort, co-ordinated by a council called the sarney which could designate an overall commander. Interestingly, the Philistine royal name "Achish" and its variants is thought to mean "the Achaian". They gradually adopted Canaanite chariot tactics, but continued to field effective infantry. Generals in chariots can always dismount as Bd (O). Some of the Philistine cities survived the Assyrian conquest as vassal states and provided levy troops for service in Egypt. Ekron became a centre of olive oil production. As on two occasions Egyptian allies arrived too late, they would be most appropriate as flank marchers.

Goliath of Gath (described in the Old Testament as fighting on foot, very large, in bronze armour and armed with a spear "like a weaver's beam" and a sword) is provided for colour and graded as Irr Bd (X). "Of Gath" might conceivably mean that he was that city's ruler. Making him a Brilliant sub-general and irregular favours his use alone as a champion (the army ran away when he lost his single combat). I suggest representing him as a figure of the next scale up, with other normal-sized lackey figures on the same base but a little to the rear. In modern times, gigantism is often accompanied by an inability to focus visually on rapidly moving objects, providing a convenient explanation of why he failed to guard effectively against David's slingstone.

30. DARK AGE AND GEOMETRIC GREEK 1160 BC - 650 BC

Warm. Ag 2. S, Rv, DH, SH, GH, O, V, RF, Rd, BUAf, F.
E: 1/30, 1/31, 1/33, 1/35, 1/40, 1/43, 1/48, 1/50, 1/52.

C-in-C: in 2-horse 2-crew chariots - Irr Cv (O) @ 16AP, or on horseback - Irr Cv (O) @ 17AP	1
Greek ally-general - as above, but 5AP less	1-3
2-horse 2-crew chariots - Irr Cv (O) @ 6AP	0-6
Cavalry - Irr Cv (I) @ 5AP	4-12
Foot warriors - Irr Ax (O) @ 3AP	48-132
Shielded archers - Irr Bw (O) @ 4AP	0-2
Unshielded archers - Irr Ps (O) @ 2AP [Can support foot warriors]	0-12
Javelinmen - Irr Ps (I) @ 1AP	4-24
Camp - Irr Bge (O) @ 2AP, or ox-wagons - Irr Bge (I) @ 1AP	0-2 per general
Triakonters - Irr Bts (O) @ 2AP [Sp, Bd, Ax, Bw or Ps]	0-4

Only before 900 BC:

Upgrade foot warriors with swords to Irr Bd (F) @ 5AP	Half

Only after 725 BC:

Upgrade foot warriors to proto-hoplites - all Irr Ax (S) @ 4AP or all Irr Sp (I) @ 3AP	All
Replace triakonters with pentekonters - Reg Gal (I) @ 3AP [Ax, Sp, Bw or Ps]	Up to ½

This list covers the armies of Greece from the recovery after the break up of the Mycenaean city states until the introduction of hoplite infantry. While chariots still appear in Geometric period art, there are few depictions of warriors fighting from them rather than being carried in them. It is thought that they usually dismounted to fight, but this is not certain enough to justify classifying them as mounted infantry. Instead, charioteers can always dismount as Blade (O) and cavalry as Blade (F) before 725 BC, and from then on as proto-hoplites. 60 chariots were still included in an Eretrian army during the Lelantine war at the very end of the 8th century BC. There are many depictions of shieldless but possibly armoured warriors riding horses, and Aristotle suggests that primitive cavalry were the most important arm before replacement by hoplites. Charioteers and cavalry both seem to wear light body armour. Foot are depicted fighting with sword (now of iron) and/or javelins, usually wearing a helmet, but otherwise naked or wearing only a loin cloth.

From 900 BC, graves contain multiple spearheads, either alone or with a dagger or short sword. Previously, equal numbers of graves have either longer sword or spears, not both. Both foot and chariot warriors are usually depicted carrying a large but flimsy, heavily convex oval basketwork "Dipylon" shield, with cut-outs on each side so that it can be slung over the back without obstructing elbows. It is because this mainly facilitates running away that we classify foot warriors as Ax or Bd (F). Other foot are depicted dipylon-shielded or unshielded with bows or unshielded with javelins. The poet Tyrtaeus describes psiloi mingling with shield-bearing close fighters. Accordingly, psiloi archers can give rear support to foot warriors, whether Bd, Ax or Sp.

Most commentators doubt that Tyrtaeus's Spartan warriors are true hoplites. Although fighting at close quarters, they use swords and javelins as well as spears, and may fight individually rather than in a rigid shield wall. Their shields cover from shoulder to shin, and there is a possible mention of a shield boss, both of which imply they were not hoplite shields. An early 7th century BC proto-Corinthian vase shows men with dipylon shields, Corinthian helmets and a pair of spears mingling with another with hoplite shield, helmet, spear and javelin and supported by an archer and a stone thrower. This would seem to imply a "proto-hoplite" transition period before the mature hoplite system originating in Argos about 680 BC had spread to the whole of Greece following the defeat of the Spartans by Pheidon of Argos in 669 BC. The change seems to have been largely complete by 665 BC, but up to 650 BC is allowed to cover isolated areas that may not have got the message.

We suggest depicting proto-hoplites by mixing hoplite and dipylon figures on the same base. Whether the mix should be classed as Sp (I) as troops on the way to becoming hoplites; or as Ax (S) as individuals in traditional kit stiffened by others in now fashionable hoplite gear but not yet fighting in phalanx, is uncertain, but Ax (S) probably has the best historical effect.

31. NEO-HITTITE AND LATER ARAMAEAN 1100 BC - 710 BC

Warm. Ag 2. S, Rv, DH, SH, GH, Wd, O, E, RF, Rd, BUAf.
E: 1/4, 1/6, 1/21, 1/22, 1/25, 1/27, 1/29, 1/30, 1/31, 1/34, 1/35, 1/39, 1/40.

C-in-C: in 2-horse 2-crew chariot - Reg Cv (S) @ 29AP, or on foot - Reg Bw (O) @ 25AP	1
Sub-general - as above	0-1
Neo-Hittite or Aramaean ally-general as above - Reg Cv (S) @ 19AP or Reg Bw (O) @ 15AP	0-3
Scouts - Irr LH (I) @ 3AP	0-1
Aramaean or Arab camelry - Irr Cm (O) @ 5AP	0-4
Camp - Irr Bge (O) @ 2AP, or pack-donkeys - Irr Bge (I) @ 1AP	0-2 per general

Only before 900 BC:

2-horse 2-crew chariots - Reg Cv (S) @ 9AP	1-4 per C-in-C and ally-general
Militia spearmen - Irr Ax (O) @ 3AP	20-60
Militia archers - Irr Ps (O) @ 2AP or Irr Bw (I) @ 3AP	5-32
Militia slingers - Irr Ps (O) @ 2AP	5-32

Only from 900 BC:

2-horse 2-crew chariots - Reg Cv (S) @ 9AP	4-9 per C-in-C or ally-general
Upgrade chariots to 2 or 3-horse 3-crew, Reg Kn (O) @ 11AP	Up to ½
Cavalry - Reg Cv (I) @ 6AP	1-4
Regular spearmen - all Reg Ax (O) @ 4AP or all Reg Sp (I) @ 4AP	0-12
Upgrade elite regular spearmen from Ax (O) to Reg Ax (S) @ 5AP or from Sp (I) to Reg Sp (O) @ 5AP	0-4
Militia spearmen - Irr Ax (O) @ 3AP	20-27
Militia archers - Irr Ps (O) @ 2AP or Irr Bw (I) @ 3AP	4-21
Militia slingers - Irr Ps (O) @ 2AP	4-21

Only from 900 BC to 750 BC:

Upgrade C-in-C and sub-generals' chariots to 3 or 4-horse 3-crew - Reg Kn (O) @ 31AP	Any

Only from 900 BC to 722 BC:

Israelite allies - List: Later Hebrew (Bk 1/34)	
Phoenician allies - List: Cypriot and Phoenician (Bk 1/35)	

Only after 750 BC:

Upgrade generals' chariots to 4-horse 4-crew - Reg Kn (S) @ 34AP if C-in-C or sub-general, 24AP if ally-general	Any
Upgrade chariots as 4-horse 4-crew palace chariots to Reg Kn (S) @ 14AP	0-1 per C-in-C or ally-general

This list covers the Aramaean and Neo-Hittite successor kingdoms of Syria and Kilikia, including Damascus, Hamath, Que, Sam'al, Tabal, Kummuhu, Ataniya and Karkemish. Karkemish was one of the few truly "Neo-Hittite" states - indeed its rulers appear to have been directly descended from the Hittite royal line. Though rich and powerful, these states fell one by one to the relentless onslaught of Assyria and Urartu, a process only delayed by their short-term defensive coalitions. Kummuhu, conquered by Sargon II, was later known as Commagene. Ally-generals do not count as of the same nationality.

The complete order of battle for the Karkar coalition of 859 BC has been preserved, as luckily has a near-contemporary list for Shalmaneser III; taken together at full scale both sides will muster some 238 chariot elements, so you will need a large table to re-create it! Aramaean or Arab camelry count as Bedouin. Chariot minima and maxima apply separately to each Neo-Hittite or Aramaean contingent. A sub-general must take his chariots from the C-in-C's contingent. The later armies of vassal or semi-independent Neo-Hittite states from 710 BC, such as the rump kingdom of Tabal, are covered by list 1/37.

41

32. WESTERN CHOU AND SPRING AND AUTUMN CHINESE 1100 BC - 480 BC

Western Chou and northern states: Cool. Ch'u, Wu or Yueh: Warm. Western Chou Ag 3, others Ag 0.
WW, Rv, DH, GH, Wd, O, BF & SH in Cool, SF & RH in Warm, M, Rd, BUAf, F. Only Ch'u, Wu and Yueh: **WW or S**, E.
E: 1/13, 1/14, 1/32, 1/43, 1/49.

C-in-C - in 3-man 4-horse chariot, Irr Kn (O) @ 19AP or Reg Kn (O) @ 31AP	1
Chinese ally-general - in 3-man 4-horse chariot, Irr Kn (O) @ 14AP	0-3
Camp - Irr Bge (O) @ 2AP, or pack-donkeys or ox-wagons - Irr Bge (I) @ 1AP	0-2 per general

Only before 700 BC:

Sub-general in 3-man 4-horse chariot, Irr Kn (O) @ 19AP or Reg Kn (O) @ 31AP	0-2
Noble 3-man 4-horse chariots - Irr Kn (O) @ 9AP	8-12
Upgrade noble chariots to Reg Kn (O) @ 11AP	0-5
Foot with short dagger-axe and shield - Irr Bd (I) @ 4AP	8-48
Foot with short spear and shield - Irr Ax (O) @ 3AP	4-16
Archers - up to ¼ Irr Ps (O) @ 2AP, remainder Irr Bw (I) @ 3AP	8-24
Upgrade Bd (I) to Reg Bd (I) @ 5AP, Ax (O) to Reg Ax (O) @ 4AP, Bw to Reg Bw (I) @ 4AP and Ps (O) to Reg Ps (O) @ 2AP	½ to all of each type
Upgrade Reg Bd (I) to Tiger guards - Reg Bd (F) @ 6AP	0-8

Only from 1027 BC to 1017 BC:

Shang ally - List: Hsia and Shang Chinese (Bk 1/13)	

Only from 700 BC:

Sub-general in 3-man 4-horse chariot, Irr Kn (O) @ 19AP or Reg Kn (O) @ 31AP	0-1
Noble 3-man 4-horse chariots - Irr Kn (O) @ 9AP	8-24
Upgrade noble chariots to Reg Kn (O) @ 11AP	0-5
Upgrade generals' chariots with 4 crew to Kn (S) @ 34AP if regular, otherwise 21AP if C-in-C or sub-general, 16AP if ally-general	All/0
Upgrade other chariots with 4 crew to Kn (S), @ 14AP if regular, otherwise 11AP	0-2
Foot with long spear or long dagger-axe - Irr Pk (F) @ 3AP	12-36
Picked troops with sword or short dagger-axe and shield - Irr Bd (F) @ 5AP	0-6
Archers - Irr Ps (O) [can support Bd (F)] or Irr Bw (I) @ 3AP	8-24
Upgrade Pk (F) to Reg Pk (F) @ 4AP, Bw (I) to Reg Bw (I) @ 4AP and Ps (O) to Reg Ps (O) @ 2AP	Up to ½ of each

Only Duke Hsiang of Sung in 638 BC:

Downgrade C-in-C to Inert general @ 75 AP less	0 or 1

Only Tsin in 632 BC:

Upgrade C-in-C to Brilliant (as Duke Wen) at 25AP extra	0 or 1

Only after 550 BC:

Replace Pk (F) with Irr Bd (F) @ 5AP or Reg Bd (F) @ 6AP	All/0

Only in Northern armies:

Jung, Ti or similar northern tribesmen - Irr Wb (F) @ 3AP or Irr Ps (O) @ 2AP	0-12
Jung, White Ti or I allies - List: Early Northern Barbarians (Bk 1/14)	

Only in the armies of Ch'u after 690 BC, Wu after 584 BC or Yueh after 510 BC:

Southern tribesmen - Irr Wb (F) @ 3AP	0-12
Dug-outs - Irr Bts (I) @ 1AP [Any foot]	0-4
Horse-rafts - Irr Shp (I) @ 2AP [Kn]	0-3

Only in the armies of Wu after 520 BC or Yueh after 510 BC:

Convicts - Irr Hd (S) @ 2AP	0-3

Only in Ch'u armies from 510 BC - 506 BC:

Stampeding herd of elephants - Irr Exp (O) @ 7AP	0-1

This list covers the Western Chou dynasty from its appearance as first allies, then rivals and supplanters of the Shang until 770 BC, and then the numerous independent states of the early Eastern Chou period, commonly named after the "Spring and Autumn Annals" of the state of Lu. It is further divided into the northern or Yellow River Valley states, including the Western Chou itself, Ch'in, Tsin, Ch'i, Cheng, Sung and Lu; and the Yangtze Valley kingdoms of Ch'u after 690, Wu after 584 and Yueh after 510. All regulars must belong to the command of a regular C-in-C or sub-general. They represent the Royal Troops of the Western Chou, or those of an exceptionally well-organised state such as Ch'i under Duke Huan, 686 - 643 BC, or Ch'u in the campaign of 595 BC. They cannot be combined with stampeding elephants.

A Chinese source says that "Shang chariots were renowned for speed, but Chou for excellence", suggesting that Chou chariots were stronger but heavier.Most were drawn by 4 horses, but a minority, particularly early in the period, can have 2; this does not affect classification, being probably due to local horse shortages. If any chariots are upgraded to (S), all generals' chariots must be. Wu and Yueh armies cannot contain more than the minimum number of chariots, or upgrade any chariots to (S). Charioteers can always dismount to fight on foot as Bw after 550 BC.

Non-guard infantry with short dagger-axes before 700 BC are classified as (I) because of their inadequate confidence and training. The option to replace infantry with Bd (F) after 550 BC represents the throwing away of long weapons to charge with the sword, a practice first recorded in a Ch'i army of 520 BC, but possible at any time after the widespread introduction of swords in the 6th century. The (F) grading is because this implies rapid advance and lacked good shields. Otherwise close-fighting infantry with long dagger-axes other than picked troops are classed as Pk (F), because these were used mixed with spears as a mainly anti-chariot weapon and also lacked substantial shields. Ps (O) can support Pk (F).

Duke Hsiang is classed as Inert because of his refusal to attack a Ch'u army while it was divided crossing a river, with the words: "Though I am but the poor representative of a fallen dynasty, I would not sound my drums to attack an unformed host".

33. VILLANOVAN ITALIAN 1000 BC - 650 BC

Warm. Ag 1. S, Rv, DH, SH, GH, O, V, RF, M, Rd, BUA, F.
E: 1/14, 1/33, 1/36, 1/14, 1/30, 1/33, 1/36.

C-in-C - on horse, Irr Cv (O) @ 17AP, or in chariot, Irr Cv (O) @ 16AP	1
Sub-general - as above	1-2
Cavalry - Irr Cv (O) @ 7AP	4-12
Camp - Irr Bge (O) @ 2AP, or ox-wagons - Irr Bge (I) @ 1AP	0-2 per general
Only before 800 BC:	
Spearmen - Irr Wb (F) @ 3AP	44-156
Only from 800 BC:	
Axemen - Irr Bd (O) @ 5AP	0-3
Spearmen - Irr Wb (O) @ 3AP	24-84
Javelinmen - Irr Ax (O) @ 3AP	16-60
Mixed archers and slingers - Irr Ps (O) @ 2AP	4-12

This list covers lowland Italian Iron Age cultures before the rise of Etruscan and Greek influence. Defence originally rested entirely on the well-to-do spearmen class with spear, sword, dagger, scutum, helmet and bronze pectoral. These fought as individuals rather than in phalanx. From the 8th century these were supplemented by poorer warriors with javelins, light axe, dagger and scutum, but rarely helmet or pectoral. Most javelins were entirely of wood without heads. Spearmen now replaced the scutum with a round bronze faced shield but lacking the hoplite grip. They continued to fight as individuals, though probably now with lower mobility. Archers and slingers were apparently few, but there are depictions of both shielded and shieldless cavalry, and of foot using two-handed axes, with shields slung at their backs.

34. LATER HEBREW 1000 BC - 586 BC

Warm. Ag 3. L, Rv, **DH**, SH, RH, GH, Wd, O, V, RF, G, Rd, BUA (BUAf from 944 BC), F.
E: 1/6, 1/25, 1/29, 1/31, 1/38, 1/44, 1/45, 1/46, 1/51, 1/53.

C-in-C - in 2-horse 2-crew chariot, Reg Cv (S) @ 29AP	1
Sub-general - as above	0-2
Scouts - Irr LH (O) @ 4AP or Irr LH (I) @ 3AP	0-1
Spearmen - Irr Ax (O) @ 3AP	16-60
Archers - Irr Ps (O) @ 2AP or Irr Bw (I) @ 3AP	4-21
Slingers - Irr Ps (O) @ 2AP	4-12
Camp - Irr Bge (O) @ 2AP, or pack-donkeys - Irr Bge (I) @ 1AP	0-2 per general
Only the United Monarchy from 1000 BC to 925 BC or Judah from 924 BC to 586 BC:	
Gibborim - Reg Ax (S) @ 5AP	4-8
Only the United Monarchy from 1000 BC to 969 BC under David:	
2-horse 2-crew chariots - Reg Cv (S) @ 9AP	0-2
Philistine and Aegean mercenaries - Reg Sp (O) @ 5AP	4-8
Only the United Monarchy from 968 BC to 925 BC under Solomon:	
2-horse 2-crew chariots - Reg Cv (S) @ 9AP	8-15
Only Israel from 924 BC to 722 BC:	
2-horse 2-crew chariots - Reg Cv (S) @ 9AP	8-18
Only Judah after 925 BC:	
2-horse 2-crew chariots - Reg Cv (S) @ 9AP	4-9
Cavalry - Reg Cv (I) @ 6AP or Reg LH (O) @ 5AP	0-2
Only Israel from 870 BC to 852 BC:	
Upgrade C-in-C (as Ahab) to Brilliant general @ 25AP extra	0 or 1

Only Israel in 853 BC:

Aramaean allies - List: Neo-Hittite and Later Aramean (Bk 1/31)	
Phoenician allies - List: Cypriot and Phoenican (Bk 2/35)	
Arab camelmen - Irr Cm (O) @ 5AP	0-4

Only Israel from 867 BC to 850 BC:

Judean allies - List Later Hebrew (Bk 1/34)	

Only after 800 BC:

Upgrade chariots to 4-horse 3-crew - Reg Kn (O) @ 31AP if general, 11AP if not	All

Only Judah from 721 BC to 671 BC:

Philistine allies - List: Philistine (Bk 1/29)	

Only Judah from 721 BC to 664 BC:

Egyptian allies - List: Libyan Egyptian (Bk 1/38) until 712 BC, then Kushite Egyptian (Bk 1/46)	0-24

Only Judah after 702 BC:

Further upgrade generals' chariots to 4-horse 4-crew - Reg Kn (S) @ 34AP	Any
Phoenician allies - List: Cypriot and Phoenican (Bk 1/35)	

Only Judah from 650 BC:

Egyptian allies - List: Saitic Egyptian (Bk 1/53)	0-16

This list covers the Hebrew states from the accession of David. The United Monarchy first ruled by Saul split into the kingdoms of Israel and Judah after the death of Solomon in 925 BC. The northern Kingdom of Israel (capital Tirza) fell to Shalmaneser V of Assyria in 722 BC and the southern Kingdom of Judah (capital Jerusalem) to Nebuchadnezzar II of Babylon in 586 BC. Chariots were initially captured from neighbours or imported from Egypt. Prior to David's reign, captured chariots and horses had been destroyed as of little use in hill country. He kept 100 of 1,000 captured chariots, and Solomon later had 1,400. After the division, Israel appears as a significant chariot power in Assyrian records but is not mentioned as using cavalry. Ahab (although denigrated in the Bible) was a very effective general and master of the short hook who first defeated the Aramean coalition of Ben-Hadad of Damascus, then headed another such coalition that successfully fought off the Assyrian army of Shalmaneser III at Qarqar in 853 BC. He was finally killed at Ramoth-gilead in 852 BC in a renewed war against Ben-Hadad when Ben-Hadad who considered Ahab "more dangerous than many a troop of soldiers" gave orders that he be singled out for attack. Gibborim "mighty men" were a knightly caste descended from David's elite guard, were armed with spear, javelin and shield and often wore armour. The Kushite Egyptians intrigued constantly with the Syrian and Hebrew kingdoms against Assyria, and actually sent an army to aid Hezekiah, King of Judah, in 701 BC, somewhat to the surprise of most parties. Attempts to reconcile the archaeology with the conventional datings retained in this book are problematic and have led some scholars to suggest that David and Solomon (and even the united monarchy) are fictional and that their achievements should instead be credited to Omri and Ahab. These difficulties largely disappear if the new datings of James and Rohl are used.

35. CYPRIOT AND PHOENICIAN 1000 BC - 332 BC

Warm. Ag 0. <u>S</u>, WH, SH, Wd, O, V, Rd, BUAf, F.
E: 1/7, 1/25, 1/29, 1/30, 1/31, 1/35, 1/41, 1/44, 1/45, 1/51, 1/52, 1/53, 1/60, 2/7, 2/12.

C-in-C in 2-horse 2-crew chariot - Reg Cv (O) @ 27AP	1
Sub-general - as C-in-C	0-1
Ally-general in 2-horse 2-crew chariot - Reg Cv (O) @ 17AP	0-3
Spearmen - Reg Ax (O) @ 4AP	24-66
Archers - Irr Ps (O) @ 2AP or Irr Bw (I) @ 3AP	8-21
Slingers - Irr Ps (O) @ 2AP	0-12
Javelinmen - Irr Ps (I) @ 1AP	0-12
Camp - Irr Bge (O) @ 2AP, or pack-donkeys - Irr Bge (I) @ 1AP	0-2 per general
Only before 900 BC:	
2-horse 2-crew chariots - Reg Cv (O) @ 7AP	4-12
Only from 900 BC to 490 BC:	
Upgrade generals in 4-horse 3-crew chariots to Reg Kn (O) @ 31AP if C-in-C or sub-general, 21AP if ally-general	All
4-horse 3-crew chariots - Reg Kn (O) @ 11AP	4-12
Only from 900 BC:	
Cavalry - Reg Cv (I) @ 6AP	0-6
Biremes/pentekonters - Reg Gal (I) @ 3AP [Ax]	0-6
Only Phoenician colonial armies in Africa, Sicily, Sardinia or Spain from 800 BC to 550 BC:	
Spanish mercenary cavalry - Irr Cv (O) @ 7AP	0-4
Sardinian or Spanish mercenary warriors - Irr Ax (O) @ 3AP	0-16
Only after 720 BC:	
Replace biremes/pentekonters with triremes/trieres - Reg Gal (F) @ 4AP [Sp, Ax]	Any
Only Cypriots from 700 BC to 380 BC:	
Ionian Greek allies - List: Dark Age and Geometric Greek (Bk 1/30) before 665 BC, then Early Hoplite Greek (Bk 1/52) from 665BC to 449 BC, then Later Hoplite Greek (Bk 2/5, from 448 BC to 380 BC.	
Only after 665 BC:	
Replace generals and spearmen with hoplites - Reg Sp (I) @ 24AP if C-in-C, 14AP if ally-general, 4AP if not	Any
Only after 490 BC:	
Regrade non-hoplite generals on horse as Reg Cv (O) @ 28AP if C-in-C, 18AP if ally general	All
Only Evagoras of Salamis' army from 392 BC to 380BC:	
Mercenary Greek sub-general commanding only mercenaries - Reg Sp (O) @ 25AP or Reg Ps (S) @ 23AP	1
Mercenary Greek hoplites - Reg Sp (O) @ 5AP	12-23
Replace mercenary Greek hoplites with mercenary Greek psiloi - Reg Ps (S) @ 3AP	Up to 12
Mercenary Cretan archers - Reg Ps (O) @ 2AP	0-4
Kilikian ally-general commanding all and only Kilikians - Irr Cv (O) @ 12AP	*1
Kilikian cavalry - Irr Cv (O) @ 7AP	*1-3
Kilikian city hoplites - Reg Sp (I) @ 4AP	*4-15
Kilikian hillmen - all Irr Ps (S) @ 3AP or all Irr Ax (O) @ 3AP	*12-36
Arab foot - Irr Ax (O) @ 3AP	0-12
Only Phoenicians in 353 BC:	
Egyptian-supplied Greek mercenary ally-general - Reg Sp (O) @ 15AP	1
Egyptian-supplied Greek mercenary hoplites - Reg Sp (O) @ 5AP	7-15
Only Phoenicians after 350 BC:	
Bolt-shooters - Reg Art (O) @ 8AP	0-6
Replace triremes/trieres with quinquiremes/penteres - Reg Gal (O) @ 5AP [Sp, Ax, Ps]	Up to ½

This list covers Cyprus until the end of Evagoras' revolt in 380 BC, Phoenician home armies until Alexander's conquest in 332 BC and Phoenician colonial armies until the rise of Carthage from 550 BC. Cyprus, due to its location off Asia Minor, was successively colonised by Mycenaeans, Sea Peoples, Dorian Greeks and Phoenicians, the resulting culture and military organisation owing more to Near Eastern models than to Greek. It was tributary to Assyria under Sargon II, Esarhaddon and Ashurbanipal. At that time it was divided into several city states - Edi'il (Idalion), Kartihadaasti (Carthage!), Kitrusi (Cition), Kuri (Curion), Lidir (Ledron), Nuria (Nurii), Pappa (Paphos), Silli (Soli), Sillu'ua (Salamis) and Tamesi (Tamassos). Some time after the collapse of Assyria, the Saitic pharaoh Amasis (Ahmose II) imposed tribute for a while. Cyprus later submitted to Persian dominion and sent forces to assist in Cambysses' invasion of Egypt. Evagoras was nominally a satrap of Persia, but allowed himself too much license and rebelled when he became suspicious that he was about to be put down, taking control of much of Phoenicia and of Kilikia. The Persians drove him out of these in 383 BC and invaded Cyprus, but he managed to cling on until political intrigues forced the Persian commanders to compromise. Minima marked * apply only if any troops so marked are used. Artillery can only be used from PF.

36. ITALIAN HILL TRIBES 1000 BC - 124 BC

Warm. Ag 3. Rv, WH, SH, GH, Wd, O, RF, G, Rd, BUAf, F. Volsci from 495 BC to 338 BC, Sardinians and Ligurians add S.
E: 1/33, 1/36, 1/52, 1/55, 1/57, 1/59, 2/8, 2/10, 2/13.

C-in-C - Irr Ax (S) @ 14AP, or unless Sardinian - Irr Cv (O) @ 17AP	1
Sub-general - as C-in-C	1-2 if Ligurian, Sicel or Sardinian, otherwise 0-1
Ally-general - as C-in-C, but @ 5AP less	0 if Ligurian, Sicel or Sardinian, otherwise 0-2
Cavalry - Irr Cv (O) @ 7AP	0 if Ligurian or Sardinian, otherwise 0, or 4-6
Infantry - Irr Ax (O) @ 3AP	48-162
Skirmishers - Irr Ps (I) @ 1AP	0-10
Ditch and palisade or rocks and felled trees - TF @ 2AP	0-12
Camp - Irr Bge (O) @ 2AP, or ox-wagons or sheep flocks-Irr Bge (I) @ 1AP, or cattle-Irr Bge (F) @2AP	0-2 per general
Ditch and bank to protect camp - TF @ 1AP	0, or 1-2 per Bge (O)
If any but Samnites, Umbrians, Hernici, Ligurians, Sicels or Sardinians:	
Replace all Ax (O) by Irr Wb (F) @ 3AP	All/0
Only if Hernici:	
Upgrade picked infantry to Reg Ax (S) @ 5AP	0-16
Any except Ligurians, Sardinians or Sicels:	
Latin allies - List: Latin, Early Roman, Early Etruscan and Umbrian (Bk 1/55)	
Only if Ligurians:	
Upgrade infantry to Irr Ax (S) @ 4AP	All
Only if Volsci from 495 BC to 338 BC:	
Triremes - Reg Gal (F) @ @ 4AP [Ax]	0-2
Only if Sardinians:	
Replace infantry with archers - Irr Bw (I) @ 3AP or Irr Ps (O) @ 2AP	¼ to ½
Boats - Irr Bts (O) @ 2AP [any foot]	0-6
Only if Sardinians from 700 BC to 300 BC:	
Mount generals in chariots - Irr Cv (O) @ 16AP	Any
Only if Sardinians from 750 BC to 525 BC:	
Phoenician allies - List: Cypriot and Phoenician (Bk 1/35)	
Sardinians in 215 BC:	
Carthaginian allies - List Later Carthaginian (Bk 2/32)	
Only if Sicels after 480 BC:	
Replace Ax (O) with Irr Sp (O) @ 4AP	Up to ½

Siciliot allies - Early Hoplite Greek (Bk 1/52),
or Carthaginian allies - Early Carthaginian (Bk 1/61)

This list covers mainland Italian hill peoples such as the Sabines, Hernici, Aequi, Volsci, Picentes, Aurunci and Sidicini until absorption by Rome in the 3rd Samnite War, Samnites before the foundation of the Samnite league in 355 BC, Umbrians before assimilation to Etruscan culture after 700 BC, Ligurians until final subjugation by Rome in 124 BC; and similar peoples of the large off-shore islands such as the Sicels/Sikels (including the related Sicans and Elymi) of the inland hill country of Sicily until 380 BC and the inhabitants of Sardinia. The Wb (F) option is because some tribes were a turbulent and hot-headed bunch, forced out by Samnite expansion and needing to acquire new lands to inhabit rather than raid. Livy mentions a Hernici army that included 8 cohorts of picked fit young men. The Volsci took Antium on the coast in about 495 BC and held it until the Latin war of 338 BC. The Rostrum in Rome took its name from the prows of Volscian warships surrendered then decorating it. Cavalry can always dismount as Wb (S). Ligurians were small but agile and strong "as bears". Early Sardinian bronze-figurines include both archers and warriors with small round shields, swords and small spears. Many have horned helmets and a few have padded cuirasses and/or small greaves. Strabo in the 1st century AD mentions short swords, peltai and mouflon-skin cuirasses.

37. MANNAIAN AND OTHER TAURUS AND ZAGROS HIGHLAND STATES 950 BC - 610 BC

Mannaia, Zamua, and Nairi: Dry. Others: Cold. Ag 1. L, Rv, CH, **DH**, RH, GH, O, E, Wd, SF in Dry, BF in Cold, Rd, BUA.
E: 1/5, 1/25, 1/37, 1/39, 1/40, 1/41, 1/42, 1/43, 1/44, 1/45, 1/51.

C-in-C in 2-horse 2-crew chariot - Irr Cv (O) @ 16AP	1
Sub-general - as above	1-2
2-horse 2 crew chariots - Irr Cv (O) @ 6AP	4-6
Cavalry - Irr Cv (I) @ 5AP	4-12
Spearmen - Irr Ax (O) @ 3AP	24-72
Archers - Irr Ps (O) @ 2AP [can support Ax] or Irr Bw (I) @ 3AP	12-60
Skirmishers - Irr Ps (I) @ 1AP	0-6
Camp - Irr Bge (O) @ 2AP, or pack-donkeys - Irr Bge (I) @ 1AP	0-2 per general
Aramaean allies - List: Early Bedouin (Bk 1/6)	
Only Kumme from 895 BC to 894 BC:	
Assyrian allies - List: Middle Assyrian and Early Neo-Assyrian (Bk 1/25)	
Only after 800 BC:	
Upgrade generals on horseback to Irr Cv (O) @ 17AP	Any
Upgrade cavalry to Irr Cv (O) @ 7AP	All
Zikirtu allies - List: Medes, Zikirtu, Andia or Parsua (Bk 1/41)	
Urartian allies - List: Urartian (Bk 1/39)	
Only if Zamua before 700 BC:	
Dry stone walls - TF @ 2AP	0-12
Only after 750 BC:	
Upgrade chariots to 4-horse, 3-crew - Irr Kn (O) @ 19AP if general, 9AP if not	All
Reclassify cavalry as Irr LH (S) @ 6AP	0-6
Kimmerian allies - List: Kimmerian, Skythian or Early Hu (Bk 1/43)	
Assyrian allies - List: Neo-Assyrian Empire (Bk 1/45) before 681 BC, then Later Sargonid Assyrian (Bk 1/51)	
Only if Hilakku after 710 BC:	
Mercenary Greek hoplites - Reg Sp (O) @ 5AP	0-8

This list covers the major Iron Age (mostly non-Iranian) highland states of the Taurus and Zagros mountains; including Mannaia, Zamua, Kumme, the later Nairi lands south of Lake Van, Shubria, Hubushkia and Musasir. After 710 BC, it also covers the independent fragments of Tabal (Kappadokia) and Hilakku (Kilikia). These kingdoms led an uneasy existence as buffer states between Assyria, Urartu and later the Kimmerians and Medes. Light horse were similar to Elamite cavalry.

38. LIBYAN EGYPTIAN 946 BC - 712 BC

Dry. Ag 2. O, E, Rd, BUAf. In Delta: **Rv**, M, otherwise **WW**, RF.
E: 1/6, 1/25, 1/29, 1/34, 1/38, 1/45, 1/46.

Egyptian C-in-C: in chariot - Reg Cv (S) @ 29AP, or on horse - Reg Cv (O) @ 28AP	1
Egyptian sub-general in chariot - Reg Cv (S) @ 29AP	0-1
Egyptian ally-general in chariot - Reg Cv (S) @ 19AP	0-2
Libu ally-general in chariot commanding all and only Libu - Reg Cv (S) @ 19AP	0-1
Meshwesh ally-general in chariot commanding only Meshwesh - Reg Cv (S) @ 19AP	0-1
Egyptian 2-horse 2-man chariots - Reg Cv (S) @ 9AP	4-21
Egyptian cavalry - Reg Cv (I) @ 6AP	0-6
Egyptian light horse - Reg LH (F) @ 5AP	0-2
Shardana Royal Guard - Reg Bd (O) @ 7AP	0-6
Egyptian Royal Guard - Reg Sp (O) @ 5AP	0-2
Libu - Irr Wb (F) @ 3AP	0-12
"Invincible Meshwesh" - Irr Wb (S) @ 5AP	8-36
Libu, Palestinian or Bedouin javelinmen - Irr Ps (I) @ 1AP or Irr Ax (I) @ 2AP	16-30
Nubian or Libu archers - Irr Ps (O) @ 2AP	4-12
Egyptian close fighters - Reg Ax (O) @ 4AP	4-12
Egyptian archers - Reg Bw (I) @ 4AP	4-12
Camp - Irr Bge (O) @ 2AP, or pack-donkeys - Irr Bge (I) @ 1AP	0-2 per general
Bari - Irr Bts (S) @ 3AP [Any foot]	0-4

The successors of Rameses III were weak rulers, and during the reign of Rameses XI the kingdom split up. By the end of his reign, Nubia had been lost and the High Priests of Amun had gained control of the rest of the south. Thereafter, Egyptian petty kings in the north were unable to resist waves of Libyan immigration that augmented the Libyans and Sea Peoples allowed to settle earlier in return for military service. Eventually, a Libyan chieftain called Sheshonq made himself pre-eminent Pharaoh over the whole of the north. The next three dynasties were all of Libyan descent but Egyptian in culture, so are treated as Egyptian generals who can command troops of any origin. They were unable to gain control over southern Egypt, which was under the influence of the Kushite rulers of Nubia and further south. A last attempt to do so led to their own overthrow. By the end of the period the north was divided into a patchwork of small principalities. Armies would then have consisted of contingents supplied by various semi-independent rulers.

The Libyan warriors of the Meshwesh and Libu tribal groups formed the mainstay of Egyptian armies in this period. The Meshwesh were largely settled in the Delta and were commanded by numerous chiefs of the Ma. The Libu settled further west and were ruled by a "Great Chief of the Libu". The command structure at the battle of Heracleopolis is preserved. It includes three kings, 1 prince and 3 chiefs and great chiefs of the Ma. The Libyan warrior elite were only finally absorbed into a national militia under Psamtik (List 53: Saitic Egyptian). Even so, they are still clearly discernable as the ancestors of the machimoi in Herodotos, divided into the two regionally distinct groups of Calasiries and Hermotybies, and as the efficient marines of the Saite and Persian periods. Up to 8 elements of javelinmen can be Bedouin. Egyptian infantry had abandoned their old shields for a round shield and some are depicted in linen corslet and either bareheaded or in a crested helmet lacking nose guard and cheek pieces which may be an Egyptian variant of the Karian helmet. These are armed with a spear and short sword and are assumed here to be guardsmen. Unarmoured foot with round shields carry a shield and two light spears. WW represents the Nile, Rv the branches of the Delta.

39. URARTIAN 880 BC - 585 BC

Cold. Ag 3. Rv, L, **DH**, RH, O, **V**, E, BF, Rd, BUAf.
E: 1/25, 1/31, 1/37, 1/40, 1/41, 1/43, 1/45, 1/51.

C-in-C in 4-horse 3-crew chariot - Reg Kn (O) @ 31AP	1
Sub-general - as above	1-2
Provincial generals in 4-horse 3-crew chariots (count as ally-generals of same nation) - Reg Kn (O) @ 21AP	0-2
Mounted scouts - Irr LH (I) @ 3AP	0-3
Mountain guides and scouts - Irr Ps (I) @ 1AP	0-3
Provincial cavalry - Irr Cv (I) @ 5AP	4-16
Provincial infantry - up to ½ Irr Ps (O) @ 2AP, remainder Irr Ax (O) @ 3AP	16-150
Reserves - all Irr Ax (I) @ 2AP or all Irr Hd (O) @ 1AP	0-10
Camp - Reg Bge (O) @ 3AP, or pack-donkeys, flocks and herds - Reg Bge (I) @ 2AP	0-2 per general
Musasirian allies - List: Mannaian and other Taurus and Zagros highland states (Bk 1/37)	

Only before 764 BC:

2-horse 2-crew chariots - Reg Cv (O) @ 6AP	4-6

Only from 764 BC:

Royal army 4-horse 3-crew chariots - Reg Kn (O) @ 11AP	0, or 4-6
Upgrade provincial cavalry to royal army kallapu cavalry [only if any royal army troops used] - Reg Cv (O) @ 8AP	4-6
Upgrade remaining provincial cavalry to provincial kallapu - Irr Cv (O) @ 7AP	All
Upgrade provincial infantry to royal army foot - up to ½ Reg Ps (O) @ 2AP, remainder Reg Ax (S) @ 5AP	0-48

Only from 880 BC to 730 BC:

Neo-Hittite and Aramaean subjects and allies - List: Neo-Hittite and Later Aramaean (Bk 1/31)	

Only from 714 BC to 585 BC:

Median allies - List: Medes, Zikirtu, Andia and Parsua (Bk 1/41)	

Only from 680 BC to 640 BC:

Kimmerian allies - List: Kimmerian, Skythian or Early Hu (Bk 1/43)	

Only after 640 BC:

Kimmerian mercenaries - Irr LH (F) @ 4AP	0-10
Assyrian deserters - ½ Reg Ax (O) @ 4AP, ½ Reg Ps (O) @ 2AP [can support other ½]	0-2

Urartu, centred in the mountains around Lake Van, expanded into Mannaia to become the Kingdom of Van, and exerted influence over the Neo-Hittite and Aramaean states of Syria. This made it a dangerous rival power to the Assyrians, and it was the subject of a number of campaigns by Shalmaneser III, Tiglath-Pileser III and Sargon II. Urartian military organisation appears to have been similar to that of the Assyrians - both probably copied each other to some extent. The Assyrians thought highly of Urartian cavalry. The C-in-C and sub-general can command provincial troops. Provincial generals cannot command regular troops other than their own element. On one occasion, the Urartians waited until snow fell before fighting Kimmerians. Crippled by Assyria, Urartu was probably finally conquered by the Medes.

40. PHRYGIAN 850 BC - 676 BC

Warm. Ag 1. Rv, GH, **RF**, Rd, BUAf, F.
E: 1/25, 1/30, 1/31, 1/37, 1/39, 1/43, 1/45, 1/48, 1/50, 1/51.

C-in-C - in chariot, Irr Cv (O) @ 16AP	1
Sub-general - as above	0-1
Ally-general - in chariot, Irr Cv (O) @ 11AP	1-3
2- or 4-horse chariots with javelin-armed crew - Irr Cv (O) @ 6AP	0-12
Cavalry - Irr Cv (O) @ 7AP	6-12
Light cavalry - Irr LH (O) @ 4AP or Irr LH (F) @ 4AP	0-4
Spearmen - Irr Ax (O) @ 3AP	40-90
Archers - Irr Ps (O) @ 2AP	3-16
Javelinmen - Irr Ps (S) @ 3AP or Irr Ps (I) @ 1AP	0-18
Slingers - Irr Ps (O) @ 2AP	0-12
Camp - Irr Bge (O) @ 2AP, or pack-donkeys or ox-wagons - Irr Bge (I) @ 1AP	0-2 per general
Urartian allies - List: Urartian (Bk 1)	
Kimmerian allies - List: Kimmerian, Skythian or Early Hu (Bk 1)	

This list covers the Phrygian kingdom of west central Asia Minor from its founding about 850 BC until its overthrow by Kimmerians allied with Urartu. Its capital was at Gordion. Several of its kings went under the name Midas (Assyrian "Mita"). The Phrygians (Assyrian Mushki), perhaps of Thracian origin, fought the Assyrians over a number of years. Tiglath-Pileser mentions five kings, so they may have comprised a group of tribes. In 709 BC they concluded peace and began paying tribute to Sargon II.

41. MEDES, ZIKIRTU, ANDIA OR PARSUA 835 BC - 550 BC

Dry. Ag 2. Rv, DH, RH, GH, O, E, SF, G, Rd, BUA.
E: 1/25, 1/30, 1/31, 1/37, 1/39, 1/43, 1/45, 1/48, 1/50, 1/51.

C-in-C - Irr Cv (O) @ 17AP if on horse, 16AP if in chariot	1
Sub-general - Irr Cv (O) @ 17AP if on horse, 16AP if in chariot	0-1
Cavalry - Irr Cv (O) @ 7AP	16-30
Spearmen - Irr Ax (O) @ 3AP	12-72
Archers - Irr Ps (O) @ 2AP [can support Spearmen]	1 per 1-2 Spearmen
Camp - Irr Bge (O) @ 2AP, or longhorn cattle herds - Irr Bge (F) @ 2AP	0-2 per general
Ditch and bank for camp - TF @ 1AP	0, or 1-2 per Bge (O)
Kimmerian or Skythian allies - List: Kimmerian, Skythian or Early Hu (Bk 1/43)	

Only before 620 BC:

Ally-general - Irr Cv (O) @ 12AP if on horse, 11AP if in chariot	0-2

Only from 669 BC:

Mannaian allies - List: Mannaian and other Taurus and Zagros highland states (Bk 1/37)	

Only Medes from 620 BC:

Sub-general - Irr Cv (O) @ 17AP if on horse, 16AP if in chariot	1-2
Ally-general - Irr Cv (O) @ 12AP if on horse, 11AP if in chariot	0-1
Regrade spearmen as Irr Sp (I) @ 3AP	All
Regrade archers as Irr Bw (I) @ 3AP	All
Armenians or similar - Irr Ax (O) @ 3AP	0-12
Parthians or similar - Irr Bw (O) @ 4AP	0-12
Kaspians or Parikanians - Irr Ps (O) @ 2AP	0-8
Kaspian or Parikanian horse - Irr LH (F) @ 4AP	0-8
Levy dregs - Irr Hd (O) @ 1AP	0-12
Babylonian allies - List: Neo-Babylonian (Bk 1/44)	

This list covers the Medes from their first mention in Assyrian annals until their incorporation into the nascent Persian Empire. It also covers other early Iranian states before 620 BC, such as Zikirtu, Andia and Parsua. According to Herodotos, Median spearmen, archers and cavalry originally fought intermixed, until Kyaxares separated them (in about 620 BC). Parsua was influenced by the Elamite emphasis on foot archery, ultimately evolving the sparabara system described under the Early Achaemenid Persian list. It is not certain at what date this change occurred, and so, to avoid spuriously differentiating between troops which may have been identical, Parsuan vassal troops in a Median army are assumed to be the same as Medes.

42. NEO-ELAMITE 800 BC - 639 BC

Dry. Ag 2. Rv, **DH**, RH, GH, O, E, SF, Rd, BUAf.
E: 1/21, 1/25, 1/37, 1/41, 1/43, 1/44, 1/45, 1/51.

C-in-C:- in 4-horse 3-crew chariot - Irr Kn (O) @ 19AP or as kallapani - Irr Mtd Bw (I) @ 14AP	1
Sub-general - as C-in-C	0-1
Elamite ally-general - as above but 5AP less, or on horse, Irr LH (S) @ 11AP	1-2
Chariots - 4-horse, 3-crew, Irr Kn (O) @ 9AP	0-2
Cavalry - Irr LH (S) @ 6AP	4-12
2- or 4-equid kallapani chariots - Irr Mtd Bw (I) @ 4AP	8-24
Spearmen - Irr Ax (O) @ 3AP	0-6
Shielded archers - Irr Bw (O) @ 4AP	0-6
Archers - Irr Bw (I) @ 3AP	36-80
Skirmishers with bow - Irr Ps (O) @ 2AP	0-12
Camp - Irr Bge (O) @ 2AP, or pack-donkeys - Irr Bge (I) @ 1AP	0-2 per general
Babylonian or tribal Aramaean allies - List: Neo-Babylonian (Bk 1/44)	
Arab allies - List: Early Bedouin (Bk 1/6)	

The Kingdom of Elam, founded around 2700 BC, was situated in what were later to be the Persian provinces of Susa and Anshan. It fought against both Babylon and Assyria, to whose reliefs we owe our knowledge of the Neo-Elamite army. How far this resembled earlier Elamite armies is unknown, except that the Elamites always depended heavily on archers. These are always depicted as unarmoured and shieldless, but an Assyrian source refers to some as "men of the bow and the shield". Kallapani were troops on fast carts, each cart carrying several archers to support true chariots or cavalry. The only depiction of an Elamite king in battle shows him riding with one of his sons and a driver, armed with bows, on a 4-horse kallapani cart. Horsemen carried long spear and sword in addition to their bow, but were unarmoured.

43. KIMMERIAN, SKYTHIAN OR EARLY HU 750 BC - 70 AD

Hu, Kimmerians and European Skythians: Cold. Central Asian Skythians: Dry.
Ag 4. Rv, GH, BF in Cold, SF in Dry, G in Dry. Chorasmians only: WW, M.
E: 1/14, 1/23, 1/30, 1/32, 1/37, 1/39, 1/40, 1/41, 1/43, 1/44, 1/45, 1/48, 1/50, 1/51, 1/60, 2/2, 2/3, 2/4, 2/5, 2/7, 2/12, 2/15, 2/17, 2/19, 2/21, 2/24, 2/25, 2/26, 2/28, 2/36, 2/37, 2/38, 2/41, 2/46, 2/48.

C-in-C - Irr Cv (O) @ 17AP or Irr LH (F) @ 14AP	1
Sub-general - Irr Cv (O) @ 17AP or Irr LH (F) @ 14AP	1-2
Horse archers - Irr LH (F) @ 4AP	32-96
Foot archers - up to ¼ Irr Ps (O) @ 2AP, remainder Irr Bw (I) @ 3AP	*12-24
Slingers - Irr Ps (O) @ 2AP	0-6
Other tribal or subject tribe foot - Irr Ax (O) @ 3AP or Irr Hd (O) @ 1AP	*4-18
Camp - Irr Bge (O) @ 2AP, or ox-wagons - Irr Bge (I) @ 1AP, or pack-ponies - Irr Bge (F) @ 2AP	0-2 per general
Wagon laager to protect camp - TF @ 1AP	0, or 1-2 per Bge (O)

Only Kimmerian from 680 BC to 675 BC:

Treres (lowland Thracian) allies - List: Thracian (Bk 1/48)	

Only Kimmerian before 640 BC:

Mannaian allies - List: Mannaian and other Taurus and Zagros highland states (Bk 1/37)	
Urartian allies - List: Urartian (Bk 1/39)	

Only Massagetae from 550 BC to 150 BC:

Upgrade generals to Irr Cv (S) @ 19AP with horse armour	2-3
Upgrade horse archers to noble cavalry: if with armoured horses - Irr Cv (S) @ 9AP, if not Irr Cv (O) @ 7AP	4-12
Upgrade foot archers to Irr Bw (O) @ 4AP	Any
Mountain Indian allies - List: Mountain Indian (Bk 2/2)	0-24

Any Skythians after 500 BC except Massagetae:

Upgrade horse archers to noble armoured cavalry - Irr Cv (O) @ 7AP	0, or 4-9

Only European Skythians in 313 BC:

Terizoi (lowland Thracian) allies - List: Thracian (Bk 1/48)	
Black Sea Greek allies - List: Later Hoplite Greek (Bk 2/5)	

Any Skythians after 300 BC except Massagetae

Upgrade Cv (O) to Irr Kn (F) [if European Skythians based as single-element wedge] @ 19AP if general, 9AP if not	All

Only Saka in 129 BC:

Seleucid allies - List: Seleucid (Bk 2/19)	

Only Hu from 400 BC to 315 BC:

Jung allies - List: Early Northern Barbarians (Bk 1/74)	

Only Tung-hu from 10 BC:

Upgrade generals to Irr Cv (S) @ 19AP	Any
Noble armoured cavalry - Irr Cv (S) @ 10AP	0-12

This covers the early horse archer nations of the Kimmerians from 750 BC to 600 BC, the European Skythians from 700 BC to 10 BC, the Asian Skythians from 750 BC to 50 AD, and the Hu of the Chinese border from their first appearance around 400 BC until the Tung-hu split into the Hsian-pi and Wu-huan in 70 AD. The Kimmerians were close relatives of the Skythians, and were driven by them from Central Asia into the European steppes in the 8th century BC. Moving on south and west, they successively broke the power of Urartu, overthrew the Phrygian kingdom in central Asia Minor, and inflicted a heavy defeat on its Lydian neighbours. They were pursued into and driven from the steppes by the Skythians and ended restricted to the former Phrygian lands. Though on occasion allied to the Assyrians, they were decisively defeated by them under Esarhaddon, and later conquered by the Medes. The Skythian king Partatua married a daughter of Esarhaddon in 679 BC, initiating a close alliance with Assyria that lasted 50 years. The European Skythians are those that pursued the Kimmerians and settled in the European steppes, soon to be cut off from their Asian relatives by the Sarmatians and in the end conquered by these; the Asian Skythians those that remained in Central Asia such as the Chorasmians of the Jaxartes delta and Aral Sea region, the

Dahae, the Saka and the Massagetae. Hu was a general term for the early mounted tribes of the Chinese border such as the Lin-hu, Tung-hu, Lou-fan and Dung-hu. While earlier mounted nomads may have made isolated incursions into China (the Hsien-yun invasion of 823 BC may have been one such) they are only known for certain after 400 BC. Minima marked * apply only to the Massagetae or if any non-allied foot are used. Cyrus the Great is variously reported to have died fighting either the Massagetae or the Derbikes and their Indian allies including elephants. We reconcile these by assuming the obscure Derbikes to have been part of the larger Massagetae confederacy. Mountain Indian allies can include 1 elephant element in addition to any elephant-mounted general. The Kimmerians co-operated in Anatolia with the Treres, believed to be Thracians. In 313 BC, Lysimachos faced an alliance of Black Sea Greek coastal cities [Later Hoplite Greek mainland minor states], Thracian Terizoi and Skythians. The Thracians deserted, the Skythians were defeated and the Greeks besieged. The Parthians tried to use a captured Seleucid army against the Asian Skythians in 129 BC, but it immediately changed sides. Only European Skythian Kn (F) can be based in single element wedge. Allied contingents from this list must be entirely mounted except for Bge.

44. NEO-BABYLONIAN 746 BC - 482 BC

Dry. Ag 1. WW, Rv, GH, O, E, SF, M, Rd, BUAf. FW from 600 BC to 539 BC.
E: 1/6, 1/34, 1/35, 1/37, 1/41, 1/42, 1/43, 1/45, 1/51, 1/53, 1/60.

C-in-C in 4-horse 3-crew chariot - Reg Kn (O) @ 31AP	1
Sub-general in 4-horse 3-crew chariot - Reg Kn (O) @ 31AP	1-2
Ally-general - as sub-general @ 10AP less [cannot command any Qurbuti guard]	0-1
Qurbuti guard 4-horse 3-crew chariots - Reg Kn (O) @ 11 AP	4-9
Qurbuti guard cavalry - Reg Cv (I) @ 6AP	3-6
Qurbuti guard infantry - Reg Ax (O) @ 4AP	0-4
Chaldean, Aramaean or militia chariots: 2-horse 2-crew - Irr Cv (O) @ 6AP, or 2-4 horse 3-crew - Irr Kn (O) @ 9AP	0-2
Chaldean, Aramaean or militia cavalry - Irr Cv (I) @ 5AP	3-6
Chaldean, Aramaean or militia archers - Irr Bw (I) @ 3AP or Irr Ps (O) @ 2AP	20-48
Camp - Irr Bge (O) @ 2AP, or pack-donkeys - Irr Bge (I) @ 1AP	0-2 per general
Flooded ditches - FO @ 2AP	0-10

Only from 669 BC to 539 BC:

Upgrade Qurbuti guard cavalry to Reg Cv (O) @ 8AP and Qurbuti guard infantry to Reg Sp (O) @ 5AP	All/0

Only Shamash-shum-ukin revolt from 651 BC to 648 BC:

Upgrade C-in-C in Assyrian 4-horse 4-crew chariot to Reg Kn (S) @ 34AP	1
Assyrian deserters - Reg Cv (S) @ 10AP	0-2
Assyrian deserters - ½ Reg Ax (O) @ 4AP, ½ Reg Ps (O) @ 2AP [can support other ½]	0-4
Arab allies of doubtful reliability [treat as ally of different nation] - List: Early Bedouin (Bk 1/6)	

Only before 639 BC:

Elamite allies - List: Neo-Elamite (Bk 1/42)	

Only from 626 BC to 539 BC:

Upgrade Chaldean, Aramaean or militia cavalry to Irr Cv (O) @ 7AP	All/0

Only in 618 BC to 605 BC:

Skythian mercenaries - Irr LH (F) @ 4AP	0-4
Mede allies - List: Medes. Zikirtu, Andia and Parsua (Bk 1/41)	

Only after 605 BC and before 539 BC:

Upgrade archers to ½ Reg Bw (X) [depicted as long-shield spearmen] double-based in front of Bw (O) @ 7AP, remainder to Reg Bw (O) @ 3AP if rear element of double base behind Bw (X), otherwise 5AP	0-28
Lydian, Ionian, Karian and other Greek mercenary hoplites - Reg Sp (O) @ 5AP	0-2
Levy infantry - ½ Reg Ax (I) @ 3AP, ½ Reg Ps (O) @ 2AP [can support other ½]	0-8
Reserves and emergency levies - Irr Hd (O) @ 1AP	0-50
Arabs subject allies [treat as allies of same nation] - List: Early Bedouin (Bk 1/6)	

Only the revolts of 522 BC to 521 BC and 482 BC:

Regrade sub-general or ally-general as mounted on horse to Reg Cv (O) @ 28AP if sub-general, 18AP if ally-general	All
Regrade Chaldean, Aramaean or militia cavalry to Irr Cv (O) @ 7AP	All
Upgrade archers - up to ½ to Irr Bw (X) @ 5AP, remainder to Irr Bw (O) @ 3AP if rear element of double base behind Bw (X), otherwise 4AP	0-16
Levies - Irr Hd (O) @ 1AP	20-60

This list covers the armies of Babylon from the accession of Nabu-nasir, through a period of nominal Assyrian rule with frequent revolts often headed by the relatively recently arrived and semi-autonomous Chaldeans and Aramaeans, the creation of the Neo-Babylonian empire under Nabopolassar (625 BC - 605 BC) and Nebuchadrezzar II (604 BC - 562 BC) and the period of dominance of the empire; until the fall of the city to the Persians in 539 BC, then the ephemeral but fiercely-fought revolts of 522 BC to 521 BC and 482 BC.

Babylonian armies of this period were usually fragile coalitions of the numerous socio-political and ethnic groups (some even strongly pro-Assyrian or, later, pro-Persian) resident in Babylonia, but based principally around the resources of the powerful Chaldean and Aramaean tribes. The Chaldeans, whose individual tribes were larger and more urbanised than the Aramaeans, eventually gained political dominance and their ambitious and talented ruling elite probably provided the final dynasty of independent Babylonia.

Babylonian cavalry in Assyrian reliefs are apparently unarmoured and do not have felt trappers. The captured Babylonian chariots of Shamash-shum-ukin have yokes for only 2 horses. Babylonian chariots in later Persian service are crewed by a driver, an archer and a "3rd man", with no mention of a 4th man. It is uncertain if the Babylonians copied the long shield from the Assyrians or vice versa. Since mixed infantry units had only a minority of long-shield spearmen, they are classed as Bw (X)/Bw (O). The Assyrians, though greatly respecting Babylonian culture, seem to have had a low opinion of the general competence of the urbanised Babylonians; but arrogance was of course an Assyrian national pastime! Nebuchadrezzar II constructed a north-facing frontier wall, the "Median wall" blocking the narrowest gap between the Tigris and Euphrates.

45. NEO-ASSYRIAN EMPIRE 745 BC - 681 BC

Warm. Ag 4. Rv, DH, SH, GH, Wd, O, V, E, RF, Rd, BUAf.
E: 1/6, 1/29, 1/34, 1/35, 1/37, 1/38, 1/39, 1/40, 1/41, 1/42, 1/43, 1/44, 1/46, 1/50.

C-in-C in 4-horse 3-crew chariot - Reg Kn (O) @ 31AP	1
Sub-general - as above	1-3
4-horse 3-crew chariots - Reg Kn (O) @ 11AP	4-15
Cavalry - up to ¼ guards Reg Cv (O) @ 8AP, remainder Reg Cv (I) @ 6AP	4-12
The "Trackers" and other mounted scouts - Reg LH (F) @ 5AP	2
Arab levies - Irr Cm (O) @ 5AP or Irr LH (I) @ 3AP	0-3
Kallapani (vehicle-mounted infantry) of the guard or kisir sharruti - ½ Reg Mtd Ax (S) @ 6AP, ½ Reg Mtd Ps (O) @ 3AP [can support other ½]	2-4
Zuk shepe (footguards)	
- until 704 BC: Reg Bd (F) @ 6AP or Reg Ax (S) @ 5AP	0-2
- after 704 BC: Reg Sp (S) [with conical shields] @ 7AP	0-4
Armoured slingers - Reg Ps (S) @ 3AP	0-2
Kisir sharruti (Infantry of the battle-array) - ½ Reg Ax (S) @ 5AP, ½ Reg Ps (O) @ 2AP [can support other ½]	8-12
Sab Sharri ("King's men") feudal infantry - ½ Irr Ax (O) @ 3AP, ½ Irr Ps (O) @ 2AP [can support other ½]	8-16
Reserves of the battle-array - ½ Reg Ax (I) @ 3AP, ½ Reg Ps (O) @ 2AP [can support other ½]	0, or 8-12
Dikut mati (levies) - Irr Hd (O) @ 1AP	0, or 20-50
Tribal levies with bow or sling - Irr Ps (O) @ 2AP	4-20
Tribal levies with javelin and shield - Irr Ps (S) @ 3AP	0-4
Siege machines - Reg WWg (S) @ 14AP	0-1
Camp - Reg Bge (O) @ 3AP, or asses or ox-carts - Reg Bge (I) @ 2AP, or camels - Reg Bge (F)@ 3AP	0-2 per general
Mud-brick and timber defences for camp - TF @ 1AP	0, or 1-2 per Bge(O)

Only 744 BC to 727 BC:	
Upgrade C-in-C to Brilliant (as Tiglath-Pileser III) at 25AP extra	0 or 1
Only 721 BC to 705 BC:	
Upgrade C-in-C to Brilliant (as Sargon II) at 25AP extra	0 or 1
Only before 710 BC:	
Aramaean and Neo-Hittite allies - List: Neo-Hittite and Later Aramaean (Bk 1/31)	
Only after 742 BC:	
Israelite vassal allies - List: Later Hebrew (Bk 1/34)	
Arab vassal allies - List: Early Bedouin (Bk 1/6)	
Only after 734 BC:	
Mede vassal allies - List: Medes, Zikirtu, Andia or Parsua (Bk 1/41)	
Only after 732 BC:	
Philistine vassal allies - List: Philistine (Bk 1/29)	0-24
Only from 731 BC to 721 BC:	
Egyptian vassal allies - List: Libyan Egyptian (Bk 1/38)	
Only after 720 BC:	
Elamaya (Elamite regiment) - Reg Bw (I) @ 4AP	0-4
Mannaian vassal allies - List: Mannaian and other Taurus and Zagros highland states (Bk 1/37)	
Only after 708 BC:	
Phrygian allies - List: Phrygian (Bk 1/40)	
Cypriot allies - List: Cypriot and Phoenician (Bk 1/35)	
Only after 704 BC:	
Divine standards in chariot with priests - Reg Bge (S) @ 6AP	0-1
Upgrade chariots to 4-horse 4-crew - Reg Kn (S) @ 34AP if general, otherwise 14AP	All
Upgrade cavalry as armoured to Reg Cv (O) @ 8AP	All
Phoenician-built biremes/pentekonters - Reg Gal (I) @ 3AP [Ax, Ps]	0-2
Phoenician-built transports - Irr Shp (I) @ 2AP [Any]	0-4
Reed boats - Irr Bts (I) @ 1AP [Ps]	0-4

This list represents the main Assyrian field-army following the reforms of Tiglath-Pileser III and before the major changes of the later Sargonids. Sargon II was the only ruler of this period sufficiently remarkable for energy and ingenuity to fully deserve rating as brilliant, the others relying on consistency and sheer hard fighting in frontal battle. However, Tiglath-pileser is also a marginal candidate for brilliance on the strength of a surprise attack on an Arab camp. The old royal household forces of the kisir sharruti formed the basis of a new professional army, consisting of the royal guards regiments, regular regiments of the home army from Assyria proper, foreign mercenaries and the corps of deportees. The troops of the kisir sharruti "royal corps" included the guards regiments, the elite home regiments of the Ashshuraya, Arraphaya, Aramaya, Arzuhinaya and Arbilaya, the "foreign legion" or Shaglute, the elite Samaraya from conquered Israel, the redoubtable Aramaean Itu'aya and Gurraya, and provincial regiments, such as the Kaldaya and Pilistaya. Provincial contingents joined on the march. The field army was divided into 5 or more all-arms corps, or emuqia, named after major deities and led by their standards. Armies were normally drawn up with a vanguard, main battle-line in two wings, and a rearguard.

The key to Assyrian success was the combination of excellent intelligence, communications and organised logistics with the superbly-equipped, well-trained and highly-mobile equestrian forces, guard regiments and regular troops of the field army. Provincial forces were small, but revolts and invasions were crushed by the rapid response this system allowed. If the field army was occupied elsewhere or in civil war, then the results were catastrophic. The large numbers of chariots are confirmed from surviving muster lists. Kallapani were infantry on fast flat-bed carts. If the C-in-C's chariot element reaches rough or difficult terrain, it can be exchanged for an extra elite cavalry element. It cannot change back. The heart land was now further north, the capital moving to first Nimrud, then Nineveh. After 704 BC, grouped divine standards may be represented in the camp unhitched as a baggage element or in a harnessed chariot as Bge (S). Guard infantry are equated with the armoured spearmen depicted with conical shields and unarmoured spearmen with flat round wicker and leather shields are equated with line infantry and classed as Ax. Assyrian armoured slingers used very heavy stones and are represented by analogy with early handgunners as Ps (S). They cannot be spearmen temporarily re-armed during a siege (since at this time spearmen other than guard were not armoured), and are unlikely to be dismounted cavalry (since these would use their bows), nor charioteers (since these are depicted as small mixed groups of archers and shield bearers). Charioteers can dismount only to attack fortifications and do so as Bw (X). Siege machines can only be deployed if the enemy has PF. Reed boats cannot be used with Gal or Shp.

46. KUSHITE EGYPTIAN 745 BC - 593 BC

Dry. Ag 3. E, SF. BUAf.
Only before 727 BC: Rv, D, Rd.
Only from 727 BC to 664 BC: In Delta, **Rv**, O, M, Rd, otherwise **WW**, O, RF, D, Rd.
Only after 664 BC: Rv. GH, V, M, D, RF.
E: 1/6, 1/7, 1/29, 1/34, 1/38, 1/45, 1/51, 1/53.

Kushite C-in-C - in chariot, Irr Cv (S) @ 18AP	1
Kushite sub-general - on horse, Irr Cv (O) @ 17AP	1-2
Kushite chariots - Irr Cv (S) @ 8AP	4-9
Upgrade Kushite chariots as 4-horse 3-crew to Irr Kn (O) @ 19AP if general, 9AP if not	Any
Kushite cavalry - Irr Cv (O) @ 7AP	7-21
Kushite archers - Irr Ps (O) @ 2AP or Irr Bw (O) @ 4AP	12-42
Kushite javelinmen - Irr Ax (O) @ 3AP	8-18
Kushite slingers - Irr Ps (O) @ 2AP	4-18
Camp - Irr Bge (O) @ 2AP, or pack-donkeys - Irr Bge (I) @ 1AP	0-2 per general
Bari - Irr Bts (S) @ 3AP [Any foot]	0-4

Only before 727 BC:

Egyptian allies - List: Libyan Egyptian (Bk 1/38)	

Only from 727 BC to 664 BC:

Egyptian sub-general - in chariot, Reg Cv (S) @ 29AP	* 1
Egyptian chariots - Reg Cv (S) @ 9AP	*4-6
Upgrade Egyptian chariots as 4-horse 3-crew to Reg Kn (O) @ 31AP if general, 11AP if not	Any
Egyptian cavalry - Reg Cv (I) @ 6AP	*2-3
Egyptian cavalry - Reg LH (F) @ 5AP	0-2
Egyptian close fighters - Reg Ax (O) @ 4AP	**4-6
Egyptian archers - Reg Bw (I) @ 4AP	**4-6
Meshwesh settled militia - Reg Sp (I) @ 4AP	**8-24
Libu settled militia - javelinmen, Irr Ax (I) @ 2AP or archers, Irr Ps (O) @ 2AP	**4-12

Nubia was lost to Egypt about 1080 BC after a civil war between its viceroy (titled "The King's Son of Kush") and the Libyan-connected High Priest of Amun at Thebes. The later partly-Egyptianised Kings of Kush adopted many of the trappings of Egyptian kingship and were fanatically devoted to the Egyptian religion. When the Libyan Pharaoh Tefnakht attempted to extend his control to southern Egypt, till then ruled by the priests of Amun as vassals of Kush, the Kushite King Piye retaliated by sending a crusading army down the Nile in 730 BC to restore the decadent northerners to godliness, defeated their combined armies and became Pharaoh of Egypt as far north as Thebes. His successor Shabaqo finished them off in 712 and extended the dynasty's rule to the whole of Egypt. A series of wars with Assyria for control of Syria followed, with eventual defeat for the Kushites, who were driven right out of Egypt in 664 BC, but continued to rule in the Sudan, moving their capital south to Meroe circa 593 BC to found the Kingdom of Meroe.

Assyrian depictions of Kushite troops show charioteers, archers, and infantry with pairs of javelins and smallish round shields. The few armoured infantry are probably officers. Nubian royal monuments show large numbers of ridden horses. Minima marked * apply only if any Egyptian troops are used. Egyptian sub-generals cannot command Kushites. Minima marked ** apply only if any Egyptian, Meshwesh or Libu infantry are used. The change to 4-horse 3-crew chariots was complete by 673 BC. WW represents the lower Nile, Rv represents branches of the Delta, or the Nile above the cataracts.

47. ILLYRIAN 700 BC - 10 AD

Cool. Ag 3. S, Rv, **DH**, SH, Wd, BF, Rd, BUA, F.
E: 1/14, 1/47, 1/48, 1/52, 1/54, 1/63, 2/5, 2/11, 2/12, 2/15, 2/17, 2/18, 2/27, 2/31, 2/33, 2/35, 2/47, 2/49, 2/52, 2/56.

C-in-C - Irr LH (O) @ 14AP or Irr Ax (S) @ 14AP	1
Sub-general - as above	1-2
Cavalry - Irr LH (O) @ 4AP	0, or 4-6
Warriors and their slaves - Irr Ps (S) @ 3AP	40-108
Archers and slingers - Irr Ps (O) @ 2AP	0-15
Javelinmen - Irr Ps (I) @ 1AP or Irr Ps (S) @ 3AP	2-15
Camp - Irr Bge (O) @ 2AP, or ox-wagons - Irr Bge (I) @ 1AP, or pack-ponies - Irr Bge (F) @ 2AP	0-2 per general
Lembi - Irr Bts (O) @ 2AP [Ax or Ps]	0-6
Paionian allies - List: Paionian (Bk 1/63)	

Only from 394 BC:	
Upgrade warriors and their slaves to Irr Ax (S) @ 4AP	All

Only in 385 BC:	
Illyrians equipped by Syracuse as hoplites - Irr Sp (O) @ 4AP	0-4
Syracusan allies - List: Syracusan (Bk 2/9)	

Only in 217 BC:	
Roman allies - List: Polybian Roman (Bk 2/33)	

The Illyrians inhabited the lands on the eastern side of the Adriatic Sea (modern Croatia and Albania). Their most aggressive period was from the creation of a powerful Illyrian state circa 394 BC by Bardylis I (who organised freebooters into an efficient army, occupied parts of Upper Macedonia and was able to place a puppet on the Macedonian throne) until the subjugation of most of their tribes by the Romans in 148 BC. Their high opinion of their own fighting qualities led to rash behaviour that got them into tight places from which only their own prowess could extricate them. As a matter of custom the Illyrians armed their slaves, who fought alongside them in battle. They were great raiders and slavers by land and sea. In 230 BC an Illyrian pirate fleet enslaved the entire population of the Epeirot city of Phoinike. The Syracusan troops and arms were supplied by Dionysius I for a campaign against Epeiros.

48. THRACIAN 700 BC - 46 AD

Cool if hill tribes or Getai, Warm if not.

Ag 1. Rv, DH, SH, Wd, BF in Cool, RF in Warm, Rd, BUA, F. Hill tribes: **DH**, BUAf. Lowland tribes: S, GH, M, V.

E: 1/30, 1/40, 1/43, 1/47, 1/48, 1/50, 1/52, 1/54, 1/60, 1/63, 2/5, 2/11, 2/12, 2/15, 2/17, 2/18, 2/19, 2/24, 2/30, 2/33, 2/35, 2/49, 2/56.

C-in-C - Irr Cv (O) @ 17AP	1
Sub-general - Irr Cv (O) @ 17AP	0-2
Peltasts - Irr Ps (S) @ 3AP [can support Cv]	28-108
Archers or slingers - Irr Ps (O) @ 2AP	4-21
Gymnetes - Irr Ps (I) @ 1AP	0-24
Camp with women, children and slaves - Irr Bge (O) @ 2AP, or ox-wagons or taunting women - Irr Bge (I) @ 1AP	0-2 per general
Palisade or wagon laager to protect camp - TF @ 1AP	0, or 1-2 per Bge (O)
Dug-outs - Irr Bts (I) @ 1 AP [Ax, Ps]	0-3
Only hill tribes:	
Convert generals to peltasts - Irr Ax (S) @ 14AP	Any
Light horse - Irr LH (O) @ 4AP	0-6
Upgrade peltasts by adding rhomphaia to Irr Ax (S) @ 4AP	Any
Only lowland tribes:	
Convert sub-generals from Cv to Irr LH (O) or (F) @ 14AP, or Irr Ax (S) @ 14AP	Any
Convert C-in-C and remaining sub-generals from Cv to Irr Kn (I) in single-element wedge @ 18AP	All if any Kn (I) used.
Noble cavalry - all Irr Kn (I) in single-element wedge @ 8AP or all Irr Cv (O) @ 7AP	0, or 4-6
Light horse - Irr LH, up to ½ (F) with bow @ 4AP, remainder (O) with javelins @ 4AP	12-32
Hill tribe allies - List: Thracian (Bk 1/48)	
Only before 320 BC:	
Upgrade peltasts by adding long spear - Irr Ax (S) @ 4AP	Up to ¼
Only Odrysians (a lowland tribe) from 475 BC to 410 BC:	
Dioi and other subject or mercenary hill tribe peltasts - Irr Ps (S) @ 3AP or Irr Ax (S) @ 4AP	0-16
Agrianes, Laioi and other subject or mercenary Paionians - Irr Ps (S) @ 3AP	0-20
Only Odrysians from 400 BC to 357 BC:	
Greek mercenary allies - List: Later Hoplite Greek (Bk 2/5).	
Only from 350 BC:	
Upgrade Thracian Ps (S) peltasts with swords and optionally larger shields to Irr Ax (O) @ 3AP	Any
Only lowland tribes from 374 BC to 357 BC:	
Athenian brilliant ally-general [Iphikrates] commanding all and only Iphikratean peltasts - Reg Pk (F) @ 39AP	0 or 1
Mercenary Iphikratean peltasts - Reg Pk (F) @ 4AP	0-16
Screen of hostages - Irr Hd (I) @ ½AP	0-4
Only after 250 BC:	
Upgrade Ax (O) peltasts to rhomphaia-armed Irr Ax (S) @ 4AP	Any
Only Odrysian Roman client kingdom from 25 BC - 46 AD:	
Upgrade generals to Reg Cv (O) @ 28 AP	1-2
Upgrade cavalry to Reg Cv (O) @ 8AP	2-4
Upgrade peltasts to Reg Ax (S) @ 5AP	8-24
Roman allies - List: Early Imperial Roman (Bk 2/56)	

Herodotos said that the Thracians would have conquered the world if they had only combined, but they enjoyed fighting each other too much to bother. They are therefore rated low in aggression. Hill tribes include the Dioi, Bessoi and Maidioi; lowland tribes the Triballians, Odrysai and Getai. Early Thracian peltasts mostly carried 2 javelins, a knife and a small pelta shield; though before 320 BC some are depicted with thrusting spears the same length as hoplite spears. Euripides listed a fictitious Thracian army as being cavalry, peltasts, archers, slingers and gymnetes "naked men", who probably threw javelins or stones so are classed as Ps (I). Thucydides states that the best fighters were independent swordsmen who came down from the Rhodope Mountains, and other writers agree on the ferocity of the hill tribes. These swordsmen may have been rhomphaia-men, the earliest excavated rhomphaia dating from the late 4th century BC, and it is also possible that they had a higher proportion of spears, since they resisted Boiotian cavalry stubbornly at Mykalessos. Hillmen accordingly have the option of being Ax (S). From around 350 BC, larger oval wicker or bronze-faced shields may have been adopted, which by 250 BC had probably been superseded in turn by the stronger thureos. Also after about 250 BC, the rhomphaia became commoner and any Thracian peltasts are allowed to be Ax (S). In 130 BC a Thracian horseman cut off a Roman general's head with one blow from a curved "sica". Famous Greek mercenary generals in Thracian service included Xenophon and Iphikrates, the possible creator of a new style Greek peltast armed with long thrusting spear instead of javelins. LH (O) and LH (F) cannot be in the same command. Arrian mentions "the women who, if the men wavered, rallied them with cries and taunts". Thrace became a Roman client kingdom in about 25 BC and a Roman province in 46 AD; its troops then becoming Roman auxilia.

49. EARLY VIETNAMESE 700 BC - 938 AD

Tropical. Ag 1. WW or L, Rv, WH, RH, GH, **Wd**, E, SF, M, Rd, BUAf.
E: 1/32, 1/49, 2/4, 2/29, 2/41, 2/63, 2/79, 3/9, 3/20, 3/23, 3/39.

C-in-C - Irr Wb(F) @ 13AP	1
Sub-general - as above	0-2
Axemen and spearmen - Irr Wb (F) @ 3AP	28-84
Archers and crossbowmen - Irr Bw (I) @ 3AP or Irr Ps (O) @ 2AP	20-54
Unshielded spearmen - Irr Ps (I) @ 1AP	0-21
Hill tribe allies:	
- Hill tribe allied general - Irr Ax (O) @ 8AP	* 1
- Hill tribesmen - Irr Ax (O) @ 3AP	*6-20
- Hill tribe archers - Irr Bw (I) @ 3AP or Irr Ps (O) @ 2AP	*4-12
Boats - Irr Bts (O) @ 2AP [any foot]	0-3
Camp- Irr Bge (O) @ 2AP, or ox-wagons or porters - Irr Bge (I) @ 1AP	0-2 per general

Only after 250 BC:

Bolt-throwing engines - Reg Art (O) @ 8AP	0-2

Only Nan-Yueh, 206 BC - 111 BC:

Upgrade C-in-C in 3-crew, 4-horse chariot to Reg Kn (O) @ 31AP	1
Upgrade sub-general to Reg Kn (O) @ 31AP if in 3-crew, 4-horse chariot, or to Reg Cv (O) @ 28AP if cavalry	0-1
Ex-Ch'in or similar crossbowmen - Reg Bw (I) @ 4AP	12-24
Ex-Ch'in or similar close-fighting foot: up to ½ with 2 metre/7 foot spear and shield - Reg Ax (O) @ 4AP, remainder with dagger axe or halberd - Reg Bd (I) @ 5AP	1 per 1-2 Reg Bw (I)
Ex-Ch'in or similar skirmishers - Reg Ps (O) @ 2AP	2-6
Ex-Ch'in or similar cavalry - Reg Cv (O) @ 8AP or Reg Cv (I) @ 6AP	0-2

Only after 110 BC:

Upgrade generals to Chinese-style cavalry, Reg Cv (O) @ 28AP	0-2
Chinese-style archers or crossbowmen - Reg Bw (I) @ 4AP or Reg Ps (O) @ 2AP [can support Ax or Bd]	*4-18
Chinese-style close-fighting foot: up to ½ with spear and shield - Reg Ax (O) @ 4AP, remainder with halberd or sword - Reg Bd (I) @ 5AP	1 per 1-3 Reg Bw (I) or Ps (O)
Chinese-style cavalry - Reg Cv (O) @ 8AP or Reg Cv (I) @ 6AP	0-2

Only after 247 AD:

Upgrade generals on elephants to Irr El (O) @ 26AP	Any
Elephants - Irr El (O) @ 16AP	0-2

Only Mai Thuc Loan's revolt in 722 AD:
(Chinese style troops cannot be used; hill-tribes are compulsory)
Chen-la Khmer allies - List: Khmer and Cham (Bk 3/23)
Lin-i Cham allies - List: Khmer and Cham (Bk 3/23)

Only in 938 AD:

Stakes planted in river bed - FO @ 2AP	0-1

The Dong-Son culture of Bronze Age Vietnam represents the ancient kingdom of Van-lang, and Au Lac which succeeded it in the 3rd century BC. Its "Lac lords" and their warriors fought with "boot-shaped" axes, spears, bows and crossbows, sometimes from the long boats depicted upon surviving bronze drums. Caches of bronze bolt-heads from Au Lac's capital have been identified as coming from multiple-bolt-shooting ballistae, though it is more likely that they were from ordinary crossbows.

Nan-Yueh was a kingdom founded by an ex-Ch'in official, based in south China but including Vietnam, which introduced Chinese military methods to the south. Its army would have been based at first on the Ch'in garrison, which was mostly recruited from convicts - hence their low status. Irregular generals cannot command regular Nan-Yueh troops.

From 111 BC until T'ang authority collapsed, Vietnam was a Chinese province, often rebellious and sometimes virtually independent under local rulers. Chinese-style troops represent the Chinese garrisons or local but Chinese-trained militia which would be available to such rulers; a rebellion of 136 AD was the first sign of such troops identifying with local interests.

War-elephants seem to be first mentioned in connection with a revolt of 248 AD. Hill tribes, sometimes called Lao, were distinguished from the lowland Vietnamese at least in the later part of this period. A hill tribe general can only command hill tribe troops and cannot ride an elephant. Minima marked * apply if any troops of that origin are used. The stakes planted as an FO in a river bed in 938 AD are best used as a Hidden Obstacle stratagem at an additional cost of 2AP.

50. LYDIAN 687 BC - 540 BC

Warm. Ag 1. S, Rv, **DH**, SH, GH, O, RF, Rd, BUAf, F.
E: 1/30, 1/40, 1/41, 1/43, 1/44, 1/45, 1/48, 1/51, 1/52, 1/60.

C-in-C - in 2-horse chariot, Irr Cv (O) @ 16AP, or on horse, Irr Kn (F) @ 19AP	1
Sub-general - Irr Kn (F) @ 19AP	1-2
Lydian heavy cavalry - Irr Kn (F) @ 9AP	8-15
Upgrade Irr Kn (F) to Reg Kn (F) @ 31AP if general, 11AP if not	All/0
Lydian 2-horse chariots - Irr Cv (O) @ 6AP	0-4
Phrygian or Paphlagonian light cavalry - Irr LH (O) @ 4AP	4-12
Lydian or Phrygian pre-hoplite spearmen - Irr Sp (I) @ 3AP or Irr Ax (O) @ 3AP	16-48
Lydian, Phrygian or Mysian javelinmen - Irr Ps (S) @ 3AP	4-18
Lydian, Mysian or Phrygian archers or slingers - Irr Ps (O) @ 2AP	0-12
Bithynians - Irr Ax (O) @ 3AP, or Thracian "swordsmen" - Irr Ax (S) @ 4AP	0-6
Skythian mercenaries - Irr LH (F) @ 4AP	0-4
War dogs - Irr Wb (F) @ 2AP	0-3
Camp- Irr Bge (O) @ 2AP, or ox-wagons or pack-donkeys - Irr Bge (I) @ 1AP	0-2 per general

Ionian Greek allies - List: Dark Age and Geometric Greek (Bk 1/30) before 665 BC, then Early Hoplite Greek (Bk 1/52)

Only from 665 BC:

Karian hoplites - Irr Sp (O) @ 4AP	0-6

Only in 540 BC:

Convert Lydian spearmen to hoplites - Irr Sp (O) @ 4AP	Any

This list covers the Lydian kingdom in Asia Minor from the overthrow of the Phrygian Maeonian dynasty in a palace coup by the native Lydian Gyges, until the incorporation of Lydia into the Persian Empire after the defeat of his descendant Kroisos/Croesus by Cyrus the Great. Suggested dates for this vary between 546 BC and 540 BC, of which this list book has adopted 540 BC

A late source, Nicolaus of Damascus, 1st century BC court historian to Herod the Great, implies that the backbone of a Lydian army consisted of paid cavalry under princes of the royal blood acting as provincial governors with the obligation of raising and maintaining provincial troops. He states that when King Alyattes attempted to conquer Karia around 566 BC, his son Kroisos borrowed great sums of money to equip his troops for the war, which resulted in his contingent being first at the rendezvous. We assume that even if the cavalry were regular, the chariots and foot would represent the levies of the nobility, so be irregular. Herodotos states that there were no more courageous fighters in Asia than the Lydian cavalry, excellent horsemen armed with the long spear. Cyrus the Great did not trust his Persian cavalry to stand up to them, so adopted the ruse of mounting men armed as cavalrymen on pack camels, and placing these in front of his infantry to frighten the Lydian horses. His own cavalry were deployed behind his infantry. In the face of this stratagem the Lydians dismounted to fight on foot, but were eventually defeated. Accordingly, Lydian Kn can always dismount as Sp (O) if the enemy army has camelry.

Polyainos says that Kroisos converted his infantry to hoplites at this time. Although he had a formal alliance with Sparta, the Spartans decided not to turn up. The Egyptian contingent mentioned in the Kyropaidia appears to have been fictitious.

51. LATER SARGONID ASSYRIAN 680 BC - 609 BC

Warm. Ag 2. Rv, DH, SH, GH, Wd, O, V, E, RF, Rd, BUAf.
E: 1/6, 1/29, 1/34, 1/35, 1/37, 1/39, 1/40, 1/41, 1/42, 1/43, 1/44, 1/46, 1/50, 1/53.

C-in-C in 4-horse 4-crew chariot - Reg Kn (S) @ 34AP	1
Divine standards in chariot with priests - Reg Bge (S) @ 6AP	0-1
Sub-general in 4-horse 4-crew chariot - Reg Kn (S) @ 34AP, or on horse, Reg Cv (O) @ 28AP	1-3
4-horse 4-crew chariots - Reg Kn (S) @ 14AP	1-8
Armoured cavalry - Reg Cv (O) @ 8AP	4-16
Mounted scouts - Reg LH (F) @ 5AP	1-3
Kallapani (vehicle-mounted infantry) - ½ Reg Mtd Ax (S) @ 6AP, ½ Reg Mtd Ps (O) @ 3AP [can support other ½]	2-4
Sha qurbute or sha massarti (footguards with conical shields) - Reg Sp (S) @ 7AP	2-4
Armoured slingers - Reg Ps (S) @ 3AP	0-2
Long-shield spearmen and archers - ½ Reg Sp (O) @ 5AP, ½ Reg Bw (O) @ 5AP	6-12
Round flat shield spearmen and archers - ½ Reg Ax (S) @ 5AP, ½ Reg Ps (O) @ 2AP [can support other ½]	6-12
Elamaya (Elamite regiment) - Reg Bw (I) @ 4AP	0-2
Reserves of the battle array - ½ Reg Ax (O) @ 4AP, ½ Reg Ps (O) @ 2AP [can support other ½]	*8-12
Levied troops of the battle-array and dikut mati emergency levies - Irr Hd (O) @ 1AP	**8-48
Tribal levies with bow or sling - Irr Ps (O) @ 2AP	4-20
Tribal levies with javelins - Irr Ps (I) @ 1AP	0-4
Camp - Reg Bge (O) @ 3AP, or asses or ox-carts - Reg Bge (I) @ 2AP, or camels - Reg Bge (F)@ 3AP	0-2 per general
Mud-brick and timber defences for camp - TF @ 1AP	0, or 1-2 per Bge (O)
Wagon laager to protect flanks of foot - TF @ 2AP	0-6
Reed boats - Irr Bts (I) @ 1AP [Ps]	0-4
Only before 668 BC:	
Mede vassal allies - List: Medes, Zikirtu, Andia or Parsua (Bk 1/41)	
Arab vassal allies - List: Early Bedouin (Bk 1/6)	
Only from 668 BC to 650 BC:	
Elamite allies - List: Neo-Elamite (Bk 1/42)	
Only before 650 BC:	
Egyptian vassal allies - List: Saitic Egyptian (Bk 1/53)	
Mannaian vassal allies - List: Mannaian and other Taurus and Zagros highland states (Bk 1/37)	
Only before 627 BC:	
Phoenician and Cypriot trieres or pentekonters - Reg Gal (F) @ 4AP or (I) @ 3AP [Ax, Ps]	0-3
Transports - Irr Shp (I) @ 2AP [Any]	0-3
Skythian allies - List: Kimmerian, Skythian or Early Hu (Bk 1/43)	
Philistine vassal allies - List: Philistine (Bk 1/29)	0-24
Only after 679 BC:	
Gimmiriya (Kimmerian regiment) - Irr LH (F) @ 4AP	0-2
Madaya (Mede regiment) - ½ Reg Ax (O) @ 4AP, ½ Reg Ps (O) @ 2AP [can support other ½]	0-4
Only after 671 BC:	
Musraya (Egyptian regiment) - Reg Bw (I) @ 4AP	0-2
Kusaya (Kushite regiment) - Irr Bw (O) @ 4AP	0-4
Only after 668 BC:	
Upgrade Cv to Reg Cv (S) with felt horse armour, @ 30AP if general, otherwise 10AP	All
Only from 641 BC to 628 BC:	
Persian allies - List: Medes, Zikirtu, Andia or Parsua (Bk 1/41)	
Only after 627 BC:	
Downgrade sub-generals to allied generals - Reg Kn (S) @ 24AP or Reg Cv (S) @ 20AP	All
Egyptian allies - List: Saitic Egyptian (Bk 1/53)	
Mannaian allies - List: Mannaian and other Taurus and Zagros highland states (Bk 1/37)	

This list represents the Assyrian field army in its final form following the expansion of the guards and other elite regiments of the kisir sharruti by the later successors of Sargon II, until the fall of the successor Assyrian kingdom in Harran in 609 BC. Although it was not immediately apparent, the empire was now entering its decline. Few offensive foreign wars were fought, civil war was becoming endemic and powerful new external enemies were arising. Generalship had discarded originality in favour of unimaginative hard fighting.

The seemingly inexplicable collapse of Assyria was, paradoxically, due to one of the reasons for its success: kingship passed to the most capable son, selected by his father the king and approved by the ruling elite, and not necessarily the first-born. Indeed, of the six Sargonids: Sargon II, himself a usurper, died in battle; Sennacherib was assassinated by his passed-over sons (whom Esarhaddon, the crown-prince, quickly defeated); Shamash-shum-ukin failed in his revolt against his brother Ashurbanipal; and Ashurbanipal's chosen son, Ashur-etil-ilani, died in battle against his brother Sin-shar-ishkun! While this system may originally have ensured able and effective rulers for a small kingdom, it did not make for a safe succession in an empire created solely by force of arms. Assyria between 626 BC and 623 BC saw three disastrously long years of ruinous civil war as the sons of Ashurbanipal struggled for power, while the Mede and Babylonian kingdoms renewed their strength. But for good fortune, the disasters of 614 BC - 612 BC could have happened at any point in Assyria's imperial history. After the fall of Nineveh, the remnants of the army retreated into modern Syria. Their new capital at Harran was lost in 610 BC and an attempt to retake it with Egyptian assistance failed in 609 BC. Nothing further is heard of Assyria in the Babylonian records, but Assyrian material culture continued into the next century in their former Syrian cities.

The conical shield carried by armoured guardsmen was greatly increased in size under Esarhaddon (673 BC - 669 BC) and a long pavise-like shield introduced for spearmen. These increases in shield size suggest that enemy archery was now considered the major danger. It has been suggested that the long shield was copied from the Egyptians, assuming that these had readopted it after seeing the shields depicted on ancient monuments. Against this, the new shield is not completely similar to these, being much larger and curved instead of flat, so it seems equally possible that the Saitic Egyptians copied it from the Assyrians. It is also possible that the Assyrians copied it from the Babylonians who also used it, but the priority cannot be established. Other unarmoured spearmen continued to carry a smaller flat round shield; and since form follows function, probably had a different tactical role. Since they were armed with a spear instead of javelins they have been graded as Ax (S) instead of (O). Although there were an equal number of archer units twinned with long-shield units, there is no evidence for combined units of archers shooting over a lesser number of long-shield spearmen, so Bw (X) has not been allowed. However, there are depictions of a small number of archers dispersed among round-shield spearmen, so Ax (S) are allowed to be supported by Ps (O).

Regiments added to the kisir sharruti during this period included the ethnically foreign regiments of the Gimmiraya, Madaya and Musraya in the reign of Esarhaddon. The latter, and possibly the Elamaya, were also greatly expanded by Ashurbanipal. These may have retained their native weapons, but this is not certain. Any mounted parts of ethnic regiments such as the Madaya are included in the Assyrian totals.

The Skythian ascendancy over the Near East, and particularly over the Medes, between circa 653 BC and 630 BC, may well have been an Assyrian use of allied troops as a deliberate instrument of policy when they could not otherwise intervene - in the same way that the Assyrians seem to have earlier used the Kimmerians against Urartu, Phrygia and Lydia. The Skythians were certainly close allies of the Assyrians at this time - indeed, the Skythian king Madyes was probably Ashurbanipal's nephew!

Minima marked * or ** are compulsory after 627 BC, but before that date apply only if troops of that origin are used. Kallapani were infantry carried on fast flat-bed carts, like those of the Elamites. If the C-in-C's chariot element reaches rough or difficult terrain, it can be exchanged for an extra cavalry element. It cannot change back. One Assyrian text describes stationary chariots and baggage carts deployed in two bodies on the flanks of an Assyrian corps as a protection against envelopment by Kimmerian horse archers. Charioteers can dismount only to attack fortifications and do so as Bw (X).

52. EARLY HOPLITE GREEK 669 BC - 449 BC

Warm. Ag 2. S, Rv, RH, GH, O, V, RF, M, Rd, BUAf, F. Unless Thessalian: DH, SH. If Thessalian: **GH**.
E: 1/7, 1/30, 1/35, 1/36, 1/47, 1/48, 1/50, 1/52, 1/53, 1/54, 1/55, 1/57, 1/60, 1/61, 1/62.

C-in-C - Irr Cv (O) @ 17AP or Irr Sp (O) @ 14AP	1
Sub-general - Irr Sp (O) @ 14AP	0-2
Hoplites - Irr Sp (O) @ 4AP	24-108
Archers or slingers - Irr Ps (O) @ 2AP	0, or 4-6
Javelinmen - Irr Ps (I) @ 1AP	0, or 4-12
Irr Bge (O) @ 2AP, or ox-wagons or slaves - Irr Bge (I) @ 1AP	0-2 per general
Pentekonters - Reg Gal (I) @ 3AP [Ps (I)]	0-3

Optionally, if ruled by Tyrant (allowed only for Corinth before 582 BC, Argos before 560 BC, Athens before 507 BC, Syracuse before 465 BC and other Siciliots, Italiots and Ionian):

Upgrade C-in-C to Reg Sp (O) @ 25AP	0 or 1
Only after 650 BC:	
Trieres - Reg Gal (F) @ 4AP [Hoplites or oarsmen]	
- Corinthian after 650 BC:	0-3
- Ionian from 499 BC to 494 BC	0-8
- Athenian after 490 BC:	0-6
- Other after 540 BC:	0-3
Oarsmen - Irr Ps (I) @ 1AP	Up to ¾ naval

Only if Spartan after 669 BC:

Upgrade Spartan C-in-C and sub-generals to Reg Sp (S) @ 27AP	All
Upgrade hoplites as Spartan citizens to Reg Sp (S) @ 7AP	12-24
Upgrade hoplites as perioikoi to Reg Sp (O) @ 5AP [can support Spartan Sp (S)]	0, or 8-30
Only if Theban:	
Theban cavalry - Reg Cv (O) @ 8AP	3-6
Only if Thessalian:	
Regrade sub-generals as Thessalian light horse - Irr LH (O) @ 14AP	1-2
Replace hoplites with Thessalian light horse - Irr LH (O) @ 4AP	¼ - ½
Upgrade Thessalian light horse to armoured nobles - Irr Cv (O) @ 7AP	0-1
Replace hoplites with javelinmen - Irr Ps (I) @ 1AP	0, or ¼ -½
Only if Thessalian from 595 BC to 586 BC:	
Athenian allies - List: Early Hoplite Greek (Bk 1/52)	
Sicyon allies - List: Early Hoplite Greek (Bk 1/52)	
Only if Aitolian or Akarnanian:	
Replace hoplites with javelinmen - Irr Ps (I) @ 1AP	¾-all
Only if Phokian:	
Buried jars - FO @ 2AP	0-8
Only if Ionian, Italiot or Siciliot:	
Upgrade C-in-C and sub-generals to Irr Cv (O) @ 17AP	All
Cavalry - up to ½ Irr LH (O) @ 4AP unless Ionian, remainder Irr Cv (O) @ 7AP	2-8
Downgrade hoplites to Irr Sp (I) @ 3AP	All/0
Only if Ionian:	
War dogs - Irr Wb (F) @ 2AP	0-3
Only if Syracusan Siciliot tyrant's army:	
Regrade hoplites: up to ¾ as mercenaries - Reg Sp (O) @ 5AP, remainder as cowed citizens - Reg Sp (I) @ 4AP	All
Sicels - Irr Ax (O) @ 3AP	0-12
Only if Syracusan Siciliot democratic army in 461 BC:	
Sicels - Irr Ax (O) @ 3AP	0-36
Only other Siciliot armies:	
Sicel allies - List Italian Hill Tribes (Bk 1/36)	
Only if Athenian after 541 BC:	
Thracians - Irr Ps (S) @ 3AP	0-4

Only if Athenian after 511 BC:

Thessalian ally-general commanding all and only Thessalians - Irr Cv (O) @ 12AP or Irr LH (O) @ 9AP	*1
Thessalian cavalry - Irr LH (O) @ 4AP	*3-9

Only if Athenian in 490 BC:

Plataian allies - List: Early Hoplite Greek (Bk 1/52)	0-8

Only if Athenian after 490 BC:

Upgrade archers to Reg Ps (O) @ 2AP [can support Athenian Sp (O)] or Reg Bw (I) @ 4AP	0-6

Only if Athenian or Corinthian:

Cavalry - Irr Cv (I) @ 5AP	0-2

Only if Spartan at Plataea in 479 BC:

Massed helots - all Irr Hd (O) @ 1AP, or all Irr Ax (I) @ 2AP, or all Irr Ps (I) @ 1AP	0, or 1 per 1-2 Sp (S)
Tegeans - Irr Sp (O) @ 4AP	2-4
Athenian allies - List: Early Hoplite Greek (Bk 1/52)	12-24
Mixed (mostly Peloponnesian) allies - List: Early Hoplite Greek (Bk 1/52)	16-36

Only if Spartan in Ionia and Thrace from later in 479 BC to 476 BC:

Athenian allies - List Early Hoplite Greek (Bk 1/52)	
Ionian allies - List Early Hoplite Greek (Bk 1/52)	

This list covers the armies of the Greek city states in mainland Greece and elsewhere from their introduction of the hoplite until that of good supporting troops. Greek tradition ascribed the introduction of the hoplite system to Pheidon, tyrant/king of Argos (possibly 680 BC - 650 BC), who used it to crushingly defeat Sparta's List 30 army in 669 BC. It then spread fast and Anatolian Greeks were providing mercenary hoplites overseas by 665 BC. Even the most backward states had taken it up by 650 BC at the latest.

Since Greek cities fought incessantly like cat and dog, an army can only have troops of a single city state unless an allied contingent is specified. A junior general is probably a political opponent of the C-in-C but not sufficiently disloyal to qualify as an ally rather than a subordinate. Allies providing only small forces are subsumed into those of the city that dragooned them.

Although Greece is termed the cradle of democracy, democratic government was limited during this era to Athens from 507 BC (with some lapses) and Ionia during the revolt against Persia of 499 BC to 494 BC. Most city states were ruled by oligarchies of wealthy landowners, but many of these occasionally (and in Syracuse mostly) were replaced by rule of a single (usually competent) tyrant often claiming to be a champion of the lower classes but requiring a professional bodyguard to protect him from the citizens.

Sparta is probably best described as a peculiar oligarchy with a pair of kings as executive officers. Spartan citizens are the Spartiate hoplite class of the city; their perioikoi are citizens of the other cities of Lakonia. They are classed as Reg Sp (O) because they were used to fighting alongside Spartans under Spartan command. Spartan allied contingents that failed to provide support on various occasions because they were delayed by religious festivals or foot-dragging, or that returned home before a battle, are not included in other nation's lists.

The Greek army at Plataea must be represented by a Spartan army consisting half of citizen Reg Sp (S), half of perioikoi Reg Sp (O), plus Tegean Irr Sp (O), an Athenian allied contingent, and another mixed allied contingent of miscellaneous states (mostly reluctant Peloponnesians) which cannot include Thessalians, Thebans, Aitolians, Akarnanians, Argives, Italiots or Siciliots. Both ally contingents count as allies of the same nationality. If a Spartan sub-general is used (representing Amompharetes), he can command only up to ¼ of the Sp (S) used including his own element and no other elements. An unprecedentally large number of helots were brought by the Spartans (according to Herodotos 7 per Spartan citizen), possibly to avoid risk of revolt at home. Although armed as psiloi, there is no mention of them skirmishing, and their role in the battle is unknown except that some died and were buried in a separate grave. Since foraging before battle is a likely employment and foragers in ancient warfare were sometimes contacted during their marauding with the risk of bringing on a premature battle, all three possible interpretations are allowed.

Athenians later thought Syracusan hoplites equal in courage to their own but less skilled, which really requires them to be graded as (I). However, since the Anatolians, Italiots and Siciliots may not yet have deteriorated with rich living, this is optional. Ps (I) in Siciliot armies from 480 BC can support cavalry. Minima marked * apply only if any troops so marked are used.

Although Thucydides says that the first trieres/trireme built in Greece was constructed at Corinth around 650 BC, the 2-bank pentekonter remained the standard Greek warship as late as the battle of Alalia in 540 BC.

Phokian buried jars can only be used as a Hidden Obstacle stratagem, at an extra cost of 2AP per element frontage.

Mounted generals can always dismount as Sp of the same grade as their nation's best hoplites.

53. SAITIC EGYPTIAN 664 BC - 335 BC

Dry. Ag 1. O, E, BUAf, Rd. In Delta, **Rv**, M. otherwise **WW**, RF.
E: 1/6, 1/7, 1/29, 1/34, 1/35, 1/44, 1/46, 1/51, 1/52, 1/56, 1/58, 1/60, 2/7.

C-in-C - Reg Cv (O) @ 28AP	1
Sub-general - as above	1-2
Greek mercenary ally-general [commanding only Greeks] - Reg Sp (O) @ 15AP	0-1
Egyptian cavalry - Irr Cv (I) @ 5AP	0-4
Egyptian light horse - Irr LH (F) @ 4AP	3-6
Guard spearmen - Reg Sp (O) @ 5AP	2-4
Guard archers - Reg Bw (O) @ 5AP	0-4
Levy spearmen - Reg Sp (I) @ 4AP	12-36
Levy archers - Reg Bw (I) @ 4AP	4-16
Levy javelinmen - Reg Ax (I) @ 3AP	0-3
Nubian archers - Irr Ps (O) @ 2AP	0-12
Libyan javelinmen - Irr Ps (I) @ 1AP	0-9
Camp - Irr Bge (O) @ 2AP, or pack-donkeys - Irr Bge (I) @ 1AP	0-2 per general
Kebnets - Reg Gal (I) @ 3AP [Sp]	0-3
Marines - Reg Sp (O) @ 5AP	1 per Gal
Only from 665 BC:	
Ionian, Karian or other Greek mercenary hoplites - Reg Sp (O) @ 5AP	0-15
Only before 650 BC:	
Egyptian ally-general in 4-horse chariot - Reg Kn (O) @ 21AP	0-1
Only from 650 BC to 600 BC:	
Remnant Assyrian garrison cavalry - Reg Cv (S) @ 10AP	0-2
Remnant Assyrian garrison infantry - ½ Reg Ax (O) @ 4AP, ½ Reg Ps (O) @ 2AP [can support other ½]	0-4
Only before 524 BC:	
Upgrade general with 4-horse 3-crew chariot to Reg Kn (O) @ 31AP	Any
Four-horse chariots - Reg Kn (O) @ 11AP	3-9
Escort cavalry - Reg Cv (O) @ 8AP	0-1
Only from 620 BC to 525 BC:	
Skythian cavalry - Irr LH (F) @ 4AP	0-3
Only after 610 BC:	
Replace Gal (I) by trieres - Reg Gal (F) @ 4AP [Sp]	Any
Only after 570 BC:	
Kyrenean allies - List: Kyrenean Greek (Bk 1/56)	
Only from 460 BC to 454 BC:	
Athenian trieres - Reg Gal (F) @ 4AP [hoplites or oarsmen]	0-6
Athenian hoplites - Irr Sp (O) @ 4AP	¼ to ½ Athenian Gal
Athenian oarsmen - Irr Ps (I) @ 1AP	½ to ¾ Athenian Gal
Only from 385 BC to 383 BC:	
Replace Greek mercenary hoplites with peltasts - Reg Ps (S) @ 3AP	0-4
Only from 361 BC to 360 BC:	
Upgrade Greek ally-general [as Agesilaos] to Brilliant general - Reg Sp (S) @ 42AP	0 or 1
Upgrade Greek hoplites if commanded by Agesilaos as Spartans - Reg Sp (S) @ 7AP	0-1
Only Nectanebo II from 359 BC to 342 BC:	
River boats - Irr Bts (O) @ 2AP [any foot]	0-6
Libyan allies - List: Early Libyan (Bk 1/7)	

This list covers Egyptian armies from the establishment of the dynasty at Sais until the Persian conquest in 525 BC. It then covers the Athenian expedition of 460 BC - 454 BC, the period from the successful revolt against the Persians in 405 BC until the Persian reconquest in 343 BC, and the unsuccessful revolt in 335 BC. Sais started as one of several small Assyrian client kingdoms in lower Egypt, but became favoured over the others, and Necho I died loyally fighting for Assyria against the Kushites. When the Assyrians withdrew from Egypt in the 650's, Sais took over under Psamtik I. According to Herodotos, the native Egyptian warrior caste supported by land grants was 250,000 Calasiries and 160,000 Hermotybies. 1,000 of each served as the royal bodyguard on a rota basis. Saitic foot formed in separate dense bodies of spearmen and archers. The first contingent of Greek mercenaries was sent by Gyges of Lydia to Psamtik. Ionians and Karians were subsequently recruited and Herodotos says Apries (589 BC - 570 BC) had 30,000 stationed at Sais. Resentment of the privileges of these foreigners caused the native elements of the army to revolt under the leadership of Amasis (Ahmose II 570 BC - 526 BC). The mercenaries fought well, but were defeated by weight of numbers. Apries fled to Babylon and was restored by a Babylonian army in 567 BC. WW represents the Nile, Rv the branches of the Delta. Necho II (610 BC - 595 BC) is said by Herodotos to have had trieres.

54. EARLY MACEDONIAN 650 BC - 355 BC

Warm. Ag 0. Rv, DH, SH, GH, Wd, O, V, RF, Rd, BUA, F.
E: 1/47, 1/48, 1/52, 1/60, 1/63, 2/5.

C-in-C - as Companions, Irr Kn (F) @ 19AP or Irr Cv (O) @ 17AP	1
Sub-general - as above	1-2
Companions - all Irr Kn (F) @ 9AP or all Irr Cv (O) @ 7AP	7-9
Peasant levy - Irr Ax (I) @ 2AP	32-90
Archers - Irr Ps (O) @ 2AP	2-6
Skirmishers - Irr Ps (I) @ 1AP	2-18
Macedonian or Coastal Greek hoplites - Irr Sp (O) @ 4AP	0-20
Macedonian or Paionian light horse - Irr LH (O) @ 4AP	0-3
Highland Macedonian ally-general - as Companions, Irr Kn (F) @ 14AP or Irr Cv (O) @ 12AP, or (if Lynkestian) Irr Sp (I) @ 8AP	*1 -2
Highland Macedonian peasants - Irr Ax (O) @ 3AP	*6-24
Lynkestian hoplites - Irr Sp (I) @ 3AP	0-8
Camp - Irr Bge (O) @ 2AP, or ox-wagons - Irr Bge (I) @ 1AP	0-2 per general
Only after 498 BC:	
Upgrade Macedonian hoplites to pezhetairoi - all Reg Sp (O) @ 5AP or all Reg Ax (S) @ 5AP	4-16
Only in 424 BC to 423 BC:	
Either Illyrian allies - List: Illyrian (Bk 1/47)	
or	
Spartan allies:	
- Brasidas - Brilliant ally-general Reg Sp (O) @ 40 AP	1
- Spartan (Peloponnesian and freed helot) hoplites - Reg Sp (O) @ 5AP	4-8
- Chalcidian hoplites - Irr Sp (O) @ 4AP	2-4
- Chalcidian cavalry - Reg Cv (O) @ 8AP	1-2
- Chalcidian peltasts - Reg Ps (S) @ 3AP	4-8
-Thracian peltasts - Irr Ps (S) @ 3AP	0-2
Only after 413 BC:	
Upgrade C-in-C, sub-generals and lowland Companions to Reg Kn (F) @ 31AP if general, otherwise 11AP	All/0
Only in 392 BC:	
Thessalian allies - List: Later Hoplite Greek (Bk 2/5)	

This list covers the armies of Argead Macedonia from the establishment of the Argead dynasty until the reforms of Philip II. Highlanders include the quasi-autonomous regions of Elimiotis, Orestis and Lynkestis. Minima marked * apply only if any troops so marked are used. Highland allied contingents can include Companions, archers, skirmishers and light horse, these counting towards the maxima for those types. Only a Lynkestian C-in-C or ally-general can use Lynkestian hoplites.

Spartans commanded by Brasidas intervened in Macedonia in 424 BC. Spartans cannot be used with Lynkestians. Thessalians restored Amyntas to the Macedonian throne after an Illyrian invasion in 392 BC.

The army relied on its noble cavalry. A coin from the reign of Alexander I depicts a cavalry trooper in petasos, hat and cloak, carrying two long spears (about 9 feet long) on a heavy horse. Thucydides describes Macedonian cavalry in Thrace in the 420s as "excellent horsemen and armed with breastplates" but in danger of being surrounded by superior numbers. The reign of Archelaos (413 BC - 399 BC) saw major reforms "in cavalry organisation and the arming of the infantry", which may have involved the state providing horses and equipment. At what period the cavalry adopted the longer xyston is unknown, but they charged aggressively at Olynthos in 382 BC.

The infantry, probably mostly armed with javelins and wicker shields, were considered inferior to the similarly armed Thracian peltasts. We assume, however, that the highland infantry accustomed to countering Illyrian raiders would be somewhat more effective. The pezhetairoi "foot companions" were an attempt to remedy this lack of good infantry and probably developed into the hypaspists of Philip II, while their own name was extended to the new pike-armed levy. Much the same arguments rehearsed over the equipment of the hypaspists therefore apply here to the pezhetairoi.

55. LATIN, EARLY ROMAN, EARLY ETRUSCAN AND UMBRIAN ITALIAN 650 BC to 290 BC

Warm. Ag 2. S, Rv, DH, SH, GH, O, V, E, RF, M, Rd, BUAf.
E: 1/36, 1/52, 1/55, 1/57, 1/59, 2/10, 2/11, 2/13.

C-in-C on horse - Irr Cv (O) @ 17AP	1
Ally-general on horse - Irr Cv (O) @ 12AP	0-2
Cavalry - Irr Cv (O) @ 7AP	4-10
Hoplites - Irr Sp (O) @ 4AP	0-48
Spearmen - Irr Sp (I) @ 3AP	40-72
Javelinmen - Irr Ps (I) @ 1AP	4-15
Slingers - Irr Ps (O) @ 2AP	2-6
Archers - Irr Ps (O) @ 2AP	0-8
Camp - Irr Bge (O) @ 2AP, or ox-wagons - Irr Bge (I) @ 1AP	0-2 per general

Only before 400 BC:

Substitute general in chariot for general on horse - Irr Cv (O) @ 16AP if C-in-C, 11AP if ally-general	Any

Only if Etruscan:

Sub-general on horse - Irr Cv (O) @ 17AP	0-1
Chariots - Irr Cv (O) @ 6AP	Up to 2 per general in chariot
Axemen - Irr Bd (O) @ 5AP	0-3
Pentekonters - Reg Gal (I) @ 3AP [Ps (I)]	0-4

Only if Umbrian:

Replace Sp (I) with Irr Ax (O) @ 3AP	All

Only if Latin after 506 BC:

Italiot allies - List: Early Hoplite Greek (Bk 1/52)	
Volsci allies - List: Italian Hill Tribes (Bk 1/36)	

Only if Latin after 400 BC:

Upgrade Cv to Reg Cv (O) @ 28AP if C-in-C, 18AP if ally-general, otherwise 8AP	All
Replace all spearmen and hoplites and at least ½ the javelinmen by Latin alae comprised ¼ each of:	
Leves - Reg Ps (I) @ 1AP	
Hastati - Reg Bd (O) @ 7AP,	
Principes - Reg Sp (O) @ 5AP,	
Triarii - Reg Sp (S) @ 7AP	28-84
Campanian allies - List: Campanian, Apulian, Lucanian or Bruttian (Bk 2/8)	
Aurunci and/or Sidicini allies - List: Italian Hill Tribes (Bk 1/36)	
Syracusan allies - List: Syracusan (Bk 2/9)	

Only if Latin in 360 BC:

Gallic allies - List: Gallic (Bk 2/11)	

This list covers Italian lowland armies from the time that Etruscan and Greek influence and city building started to modify the Villanovan culture. It includes the Etruscans from the introduction of the hoplite until the founding shortly after of the Etruscan league circa 600 BC and Rome until the reforms of Servius Tullius circa 578 BC, these armies then being covered by their own lists. The list then continues to cover Latin armies until the destruction of the Latin League in 338 BC and Umbrian armies until the end of the 3rd Samnite War in 290 BC. Very little non-archaeological information is available on any of these armies, but we postulate that cavalry remained an important arm, and that somewhat steadier peasant spearmen with scutum were being supplemented by a class of wealthy hoplites. By 400 BC, Latin armies were probably assimilated to the Roman model, but possibly had more cavalry. Campanian allies cannot include Cv except for the general's element.

56. KYRENEAN GREEK 630 BC - 74 BC

Dry. Ag 0. S, DH, WH, GH, Wd, O, SF, D, G, Rd, BUAf, F.
E: 1/7, 1/53, 1/60, 1/61, 2/7, 2/12, 2/20.

C-in-C: on horse - Irr Cv (I) @ 15AP, or as hoplite, Irr Sp (O) @ 14AP	1
Sub-general - as above	1-2
Cavalry- Irr Cv (I) @ 5AP	0-3
Hoplites - Irr Sp (O) @ 4AP	36-72
To transport generals or hoplites on light carts as mounted infantry @ +1AP	Any
Archers and slingers - Irr Ps (O) @ 2AP	0-12
Javelinmen - Irr Ps (I) @ 1AP	0-36
Camp - Irr Bge (O) @ 2AP, or pack-donkeys - Irr Bge (I) @ 1AP	0-2 per general
Ditch and/or palisade to defend camp - TF @ 1AP	0, or 1-2 per Bge (O)
Ditch and/or palisade as field defences - TF @ 2AP	0-6
Trieres - Reg Gal (F) @ 4 AP [any foot]	0-1
Libyan allies - List: Early Libyan (Bk 1/7)	
Only before 275 BC:	
Upgrade generals if in 4-horse chariots to Irr Cv (O) @ 16AP	Any
Four-horse chariots with javelin-armed crew - Irr Cv (O) @ 6AP	4-10
Only in 322 BC:	
Carthaginian allies - List: Early Carthaginian (Bk 1/61)	
Only from 313 BC to 308 BC:	
Upgrade C-in-C to Reg Kn (F) in single-element wedge @ 31AP	1
Mercenary sub-general - Reg Sp (O) @ 25AP or Reg Cv (O) @ 28AP	0-1
Ophellas' companions in single-element wedge - Reg Kn (F) @ 11AP	0-1
Mercenary or Athenian cavalry - Reg Cv (O) @ 8AP	0-2
Macedonian pikemen - Reg Pk (O) @ 4AP	4-8
Mercenary peltasts - Reg Ax (O) @ 4AP	0-8
Mercenary archers and slingers - Reg Ps (O) @ 2AP	0-8
Ophellas' Athenian volunteers - Reg Sp (O) @ 5AP	8-24
Only after 308 BC:	
Convert C-in-C to Reg Kn (F) in single-element wedge @ 31AP	0-1
Ptolemaic ruler's household cavalry - Reg Kn (F) in single-element wedge @ 11AP	0-3
Ptolemaic ruler's household infantry - Reg Ax (S) @ 5AP or Reg Pk (S) @ 5AP	0-4
Cretan mercenaries - Reg Ps (O) @ 2AP	0-8
Other mercenaries - Reg Ax (S) @ 5AP or Reg Pk (O) @ 4AP	0-8
Only from 275 BC:	
Upgrade Cv (I) to Irr Cv (O) @ 17AP if C-in-C or sub-general, 7AP if not	Any

Kyrene was the largest of several Greek colonies in the Cyrenaica region of modern Libya. This list covers Kyrenean armies from the city's foundation until its annexation by Rome. Kyrene was noted for copying four-horsed chariots from the neighbouring Libyans, and for transporting hoplites in carts to prevent fatigue (and, in North Africa, perhaps thirst).

In 322 BC, Kyrene mustered Libyan and Carthaginian allies in a domestic dispute, but ended up being annexed by Ptolemy of Egypt. His Macedonian governor Ophellas soon set up as an independent ruler; and in 308 BC took a Kyrenean army including many Athenian volunteers to join Agathokles of Syracuse against Carthage. Agathokles had him killed and took over his army. A Kyrenian allied contingent for Agathocles in 308 BC can include companions, up to 2 elements of Athenian Cv (O) and up to 4 Macedonian pikemen elements. Thereafter Kyrene was attached to Ptolemaic Egypt, sometimes as an independent state under a king of the Ptolemaic house, until Ptolemy Apion bequeathed it to Rome.

Ptolemy Physkon hired mercenaries including 1,000 Cretans in 163 BC, and although Polybios describes him being defeated by the Kyreneans (after putting their Libyan allies to flight) he did eventually regain control of Kyrene. The Spartan force that made a fleeting appearance and intervened in a local siege in 414 BC when blown off-course sailing to reinforce Syracuse is not included. A collection of stratagems mentions Kyrenean women digging military ditches on one occasion, which at least attests the possibility of TF.

57. ETRUSCAN LEAGUE 600 BC - 280 BC

Warm. Ag 3. S, Rv, DH, SH, GH, O, V, E, RF, M, Rd, BUAf.
E: 1/36, 1/52, 1/55, 1/59, 2/8, 2/9, 2/10, 2/11, 2/13.

C-in-C on horse - Reg Cv (O) @ 28AP	1
Sub-general - as above	0-1
Etruscan ally-general on horse - Reg Cv (O) @ 18AP	0-3
Raiding light horse - Irr LH (O) @ 4AP	0-2
Cavalry - Reg Cv (O) @ 8AP	4-7
Hoplites - Reg Sp (O) @ 5AP	8-12
2nd and 3rd class - Reg Sp (I) @ 4AP	20-75
Option to replace both hoplites and 2nd and 3rd class with hoplites - Reg Sp (I) @ 4AP	All/0
Upgrade hoplites as "Devoted" to Reg Sp (S) @ 7AP	Up to 1 per general
Axemen - Reg Bd (O) @ 7AP	Up to 1 per general
Archers and slingers - Reg Ps (O) @ 2AP	4-8
Javelinmen - Irr Ps (I) @ 1AP	8-24
Peasant militia - Irr Hd (O) @ 1AP	0-10
Camp - Irr Bge (O) @ 2AP, or ox-wagons - Irr Bge (I) @ 1AP	0-2 per general
Ditch and bank to protect camp - TF @ 1AP	0, or 1-2 per Bge (O)
Italiot allies - List: Early Hoplite Greek (Bk 1/52) or Later Hoplite Greek (Bk 2/5)	
Sabine allies - List: Italian Hill Tribes (Bk 1/36)	
Umbrian allies - List: Latin, Early Roman, Early Etruscan and Umbrian (Bk 1/55)	
Samnite allies - List: Samnite (Bk 2/13)	
Italian hill tribe allies - List: Italian Hill Tribes (Bk 1/36), or Gallic allies - List: Gallic (Bk 2/11)	
Only before 500 BC:	
Downgrade general in 2- or 4-horse 2-crew chariot to Reg Cv (O) @ 27AP if C-in-C or sub-general, 17AP if ally-general	All unless no chariots used
2-horse 2-crew chariots - Reg Cv (O) @ 7AP	Up to 2 per general
Pentekonters - Reg Gal (I) @ 3AP [Sp or Ps (I)]	0-4
Latin allies - List: Latin, Early Roman, Early Etruscan and Umbrian (Bk 1/55)	
Only from 550 BC to 450 BC:	
Carthaginian triremes - Reg Gal (F) @ 4AP [Ax]	0-2
Carthaginian marines - Reg Ax (O) @ 4AP	1 per Carthaginian Gal
Only from 506 BC to 500 BC:	
Roman allies - List: Tullian Roman (Bk 1/59)	
Only from 500 BC to 474 BC:	
Triremes - Reg Gal (F) @ 4AP [Reg Sp]	0-4
Only after 400 BC:	
Re-arm hoplites with pila - Reg Bd (I) @ 5AP	¼ to ½
Only in 357 BC:	
Fanatic priests waving snakes and burning torches - Irr Hd (S) @ 2AP	0-1
Only in 310 BC:	
Regrade hoplites with pila as Irr Bd (O) @ 5AP	All

This list covers Etruscan armies from the founding of the Etruscan league until subjection by Rome. Any sizeable army had to be provided by several of the allied cities. The Romans were said by Livy to have feared the Etruscans for their numbers rather than their skill or courage. A modern Italian source suggests that the backbone of the army was a regular force of armoured Greek-style hoplites kept permanently in arms, supported in time of war by greater numbers of 2nd and 3rd class spearmen largely lacking body armour and with the oval scutum as their shield. A 4th class provided skirmishers. Since their Villanovan predecessors combined such troops with others carrying round metal shields, and the Etruscans were only the upper stratum of a mixed society, this is not implausible, but direct evidence for the theory is lacking, so the traditional view is also provided as an option. Unlike the Romans, the army fought in a single line with each general's hoplites flanked by his 2nd and 3rd class. It is not certain that the "Devoted" troops, picked from the best and sworn by a special religious rite to die rather than retire, were hoplites. They might have been generals' cavalry escorts or the axemen. They were used as a reserve to repair penetrations of the front line or cover a retreat. Special units of armoured men with two-handed axes were used to create or exploit breakthroughs. Etruscan seapower was pre-eminent in the north-western Mediterranean until it was broken at

Cumae by Syracuse in 474 BC. Marines were provided by the hoplites. The use of chariots other than by generals is doubtful. Chariotry can always dismount to fight on foot as Reg Sp (S), and cavalry as Reg Ax (S). Lighter horse were used mainly for raiding. Snake- and firebrand-waving priests used on one occasion in 357 BC against the Romans caused momentary dismay before being cut down. At another battle in 310 BC, an army picked by the unusual method of selection by buddies surprised the Romans by charging with swords without throwing missiles and fighting much harder than expected from Etruscans. Non-Etruscan allies cannot be used in 310 BC. Otherwise Umbrian, Samnite and Gallic allies can be used together. Neither Italiot allies nor Carthaginians can be used with other non-Etruscan allies, nor with each other. Latin and Roman allies cannot be used together.

58. MEROITIC KUSHITE 592 BC - 350 AD

Dry. Ag 1. Rv, GH, E, SF, M, D, BUA.
E: 1/53, 1/60, 2/20, 2/55, 2/56, 2/62, 2/64.

C-in-C - Irr Cv (O) @ 17AP or Irr Bw (O) @ 14AP	1
Sub-general - as above	1-2
Meroitic cavalry - Irr Cv (O) @ 7AP	0-12
Meroitic archers - Irr Bw (O) @ 4AP	12-24
Tribal spearmen - Irr Sp (I) @ 3AP	30-80
Tribal axemen and swordsmen - Irr Bd (I) @ 4AP	8-30
Tribal archers - Irr Bw (I) @ 3AP	0-20
Upgrade tribal archers to Irr Bw (O) @ 4AP	Up to ¼
Trogodyte skirmishing archers - Irr Ps (O) @ 2AP	0-12
Dug-outs - Irr Bts (I) @ 1AP [Sp, Bd, Bw or Ps]	0-1
Camp - Irr Bge (O) @ 2AP, or pack-donkeys - Irr Bge (I) @ 1AP	0-2 per general

Only after 300 BC:

Upgrade C-in-C mounted on elephant to Irr El (I) @ 22AP	0-1
African elephants - Irr El (I) @ 12AP	0-2
Desert Blemmye subject allies - List: Nobades, Blemmye or Beja (Bk 2/55)	

Only from 27 BC to 22 BC:

Downgrade C-in-C (as Queen Amanirenas) to Inert general @ 75AP less.	0 or 1

Some time after the Kushite withdrawal from Egypt the capital of Kush, Napata, was destroyed by the Saitic pharaoh Psamtik II, and a new capital was established to the south at Meroe. The kingdom, known as "Aithiopia" in Greek sources, was still under heavy Egyptian cultural influence and was frequently ruled by the Queen Mother with the title Candace. An Achaemenid invasion under Cambysses perished in the desert; Meroitic kings supported some of the Egyptian revolts against the Ptolemies; early Imperial Roman forces defeated Meroitic raiders and sacked Napata in a punitive expedition. The kingdom, weakened by attacks from the Noba, or Nobades, fell to the Abyssinian kingdom of Axum in about 350 AD. Strabo describes its forces as poorly equipped and poorly marshalled spearmen with large hide shields, plus axemen and swordsmen; Meroitic art suggests some better-equipped archers were available from the core of the kingdom, armed with axe, sword or spear in addition to bow and there are Ptolemaic figurines with axe and shield only. There is evidence for war elephants, presumably inspired by Ptolemaic practice. Trogodytes (corrupted to Troglodytes) were not cave-dwellers as the latter implies, but nomadic herdsmen described as "lightly clad in skins" and mainly fighting with bows. Amanirenas is sometimes called Candace, actually her title.

59. TULLIAN ROMAN 578 BC - 400 BC

Warm. Ag 2. S. Rv, DH, SH, GH, O, V, E, RF, M, Rd, BUAf.
E: 1/36, 1/55, 1/57, 2/8.

Roman C-in-C - Reg Cv (O) @ 28AP or Reg Sp (S) @ 27AP	1
Roman sub-general - Reg Cv (O) @ 28AP	1-3 if no ally-general used
Equites - Reg Cv (O) @ 8AP	1 per 4-8 Sp (I)
1st class - Irr Sp (O) @ 4AP	1-2 per 2 Sp (I)
2nd and 3rd classes - Irr Sp (I) @ 3AP [can support Sp (O)]	16-64
4th class - all Irr Ax (I) @ 2AP or all Irr Ax (O) @ 3AP	1-2 per 2 Sp (I)
5th class - all Irr Ps (O) @ 2AP, or ½ Irr Ps (O) @ 2AP, ½ Irr Ps (I) @ 1AP	1-3 per 2 Sp (I)
Camp - Irr Bge (O) @ 2AP, or ox-wagons - Irr Bge (I) @ 1AP	0-2 per general
Ditch and palisade to defend camp - TF @ 1AP	0, or 1-2 per Bge (O)

Only after 509 BC:

Roman ally-general - Reg Cv (O) @ 18AP or Reg Sp (S) @ 17AP	0-1
Latin allies - List Latin, Early Roman, Early Etruscan and Umbrian Italian (Bk 1/55)	Up to 2 contingents
Hernician allies - List: Italian Hill Tribes (Bk 1/36)	

This list covers the armies of Rome from the reforms of Servius Tullius until those of Camillus. Until 509 BC, the C-in-C represents the king and 1 or 2 sub-generals his sons. After 509 BC, the C-in-C can either represent the senior of the two Consuls, in which case he must be assisted by the other Consul as a Roman ally-general; or a temporary Dictator, in which case he must be assisted by his Master of the Horse and one or both Consuls as Roman sub-generals. Although equites were centrally equipped and maintained, the foot were an unpaid militia, but described by Livy as organised into centuries by class, performing simple manoeuvres on the battlefield and frequently pressing their officers to provide more aggressive orders rather than charging disobediently. It seems best to class them as irregular but under regular generals. The 1st class were equipped as armoured hoplites. The 2nd and 3rd class had the oval scutum as their shield instead of the round hoplon or aspis and had only minimal armour. The 4th class are described by Livy as having spear and javelins but no shield, but by Dionysios as also having shields. Livy describes the 5th class as slingers, Dionysios as slingers and javelinmen. Under the kings, each maniple combined a Roman and a Latin century. Under the republic from 509 BC, Latins had either been granted citizenship, or were so much under the thumb that they were not allowed to fight at all, or if independent were reluctant to serve and did so if at all in separate contingents under their own generals. Equites can always dismount to fight on foot as Ax (S).

60. EARLY ACHAEMENID PERSIAN 550 BC - 420 BC

Dry. Ag 3. Rv, DH, RH, GH, O, SF, RF, G, Rd, BUAf, F. Only after 540 BC: WW, E.
E: 1/6, 1/7, 1/8, 1/23, 1/35, 1/41, 1/43, 1/44, 1/48, 1/50, 1/52, 1/53, 1/54, 1/56, 1/58, 1/62, 1/63, 2/1, 2/2, 2/3, 2/5, 2/6.

C-in-C - Reg Cv (O) @ 27AP if in 2-horse chariot, 28AP if on horse	1
Sub-general - Reg Cv (O) @ 27AP if in 2-horse chariot, 28AP if on horse	1-2
Replace Bge (O) with sacred standard in chariot drawn by 4 white Nisaean horses - Irr Bge (S) @ 3AP	0 or 1
Guard cavalry - Reg Cv (O) @ 8AP	0-2
Persian, Median, Bactrian or similar cavalry - Irr Cv (O) @ 7AP	6-12
Immortals - double-based Reg Bw, front rank (X) @ 7AP, rear rank (O) @ 3AP	*6-12
Other sparabara foot - double-based Irr Bw, front rank (X) @ 5AP, rear rank (O) @ 3AP	12-36
Kaspian, Skythian or similar cavalry - Irr LH (F) @ 4AP	**2-8
Sagartian lasso-men - Irr LH (O) @ 4AP	0-2
Armenians, Paphlagonians or similar - Irr Ax (O) @ 3AP	**2-8
Kaspian, Parikanian or similar archers - Irr Ps (O) @ 2AP	0-8
Parthian, Bactrian, Skythian or similar archers - Irr Bw (O) @ 4AP	**2-8
Levy dregs - Irr Hd (O) @ 1AP	0-20
Camp - Irr Bge (O) @ 2AP, or pack-donkeys - Irr Bge (I) @ 1AP, or pack-camels - Irr Bge (F) @ 2 A P	0-2 per general
Palisade to protect camp - TF @ 1AP	0, or 1-2 per Bge(O)
Rafts of inflated skins - Irr Bts (I) @ 1AP [any foot]	0-6
Only in 550 BC:	
Mede rebel allies - List: Medes, Zikirtu, Andia or Parsua (Bk 1/41)	
Only from 550 BC to 520 BC:	
Saka allies - List: Kimmerian, Skythian or Early Hu (Bk 1/43)	
Only in 540 BC:	
Cyrus' camelry - Irr Cm (O) @ 5AP	***2-5
Cyrus' scythed chariots - Irr Exp (O) @ 7AP	***2-3
Cyrus' mobile towers - Irr WWg (S) @ 10AP	***1-3
Only 539 BC to 500 BC:	
Babylonian 4 horse chariots - Reg Kn (O) @ 11AP	0-1 per 2 Chaldean foot
Only from 539 BC:	
Mysians, Pisidians, Bithynians or similar - Irr Ps (S) @ 3AP	**2-8
Milyan javelinmen and archers - up to ½ Irr Ps (O) @ 2AP, remainder Irr Ps (I) @ 1AP	0-4
Lydian or Ionian hoplites - Irr Sp (I) @ 3AP	0-6
Assyrian foot - Reg Sp (I) @ 4AP	0-8
Chaldean foot - Reg Bw (I) @ 4AP or Reg Ps (O) @ 2AP [can support Assyrian Sp (I)]	0-8
Bedouin camelry - Irr Cm (O) @ 5AP or Irr LH (I) @ 3AP	0-2
Triremes - Reg Gal (F) @ 4AP [Phoenician Ax, Ionian Sp, Lykian Bw]	0-4
Lykian marines - Irr Bw (O) @ 4AP	Up to 1 per 4 Gal
Only after 539 BC:	
Phoenician marines - Reg Ax (O) @ 4AP	Up to 1 per Gal
Only after 526 BC:	
Libyan javelinmen - Irr Ps (I) @ 1AP	0 or 4-8
Libyan chariots - Irr Cv (O) @ 6AP	0-1 per 4 Libyan Ps (I)
Indian infantry - Irr Bw (O) @ 4AP	0, or 2-4
Indian chariots - Irr Cv (S) @ 8AP	0-1 per 2 Indian Bw (O)
Egyptian marines - Reg Sp (O) @ 5AP	0-3
Egyptian triremes - Reg Gal (F) @ 4AP [Egyptian marines]	0-3
Transports - Irr Shp (I) @ 2AP [Cv or Bge]	0-8
Only from 492 BC to 479 BC:	
Upgrade C-in-C to Brilliant (as Mardonios) at 25AP extra	0 or 1
Only from 492 BC to 466 BC:	
European Thracians - up to ½ hillmen Irr Ax (S) @ 4AP remainder Irr Ps (S) @ 3AP	0-4
Only in 479 BC in Greece:	
Medizing Greek Theban ally-general [commanding all Thebans and only Greeks] - Irr Sp (O) @ 9AP	1
Medizing Greek Theban cavalry - Reg Cv (O) @ 8AP	1-2
Medizing Greek Thessalian horsemen - Irr LH (O) @ 4AP	0-3

Medizing Greek Theban hoplites - Irr Sp (O) @ 4AP	7-11
Other medizing but unenthusiastic Greek hoplites mainly from Phokis and Thessaly - Irr Sp (I) @ 3A P	4-8
Medizing Greek javelinmen - Irr Ps (I) @ 1AP	4-8
Medizing Greek Macedonians - Irr Ax (I) @ 2AP	0-4

Only from 465 BC to 449 BC:

Replace sparabara foot with crescent-shielded archers - Immortals as Reg Bw (O) @ 5AP or Reg Ps (O) @ 2AP, others as Irr Bw (O) @ 4AP or Irr Ps (O) @ 2AP	Up to ¼

Only after 449 BC:

Replace sparabara with up to ¼ takabara peltasts - Immortals as Reg Ax (O) @ 4AP,others as Irr Ax (O) @ 3AP, remainder with crescent-shield archers as above [if Ps can support takabara]	½ to all

This list covers Achaemenid Persian armies from Cyrus the Great's defeat of the Medes until the abandonment of sparabara infantry. The current view is that the Immortals and other Persian line infantry at the time of the invasions of Greece were organised with a front rank of men armed with spear and a pavise-sized cane and leather shield (called a gerrhon in Greek and spara in Persian), followed by nine ranks without shields armed with bow and spear; the combination being referred to here as sparabara. The minimum marked * applies only if any Immortals are used, in which case 6 can be deducted from the minimum number of other sparabara foot. Minima marked ** apply if any troops so marked are used. Most such troops are taken from Herodotos' list of those taking part in Xerxes invasion of Greece. Other troops specified by him as equivalent can be substituted, with the same classification and cost.

Troops marked *** are ascribed by Xenophon to Cyrus the Great as created for a battle that took place sometime between 546 BC and 540 BC. This list assumes it was in 540 BC. The towers are probably fictional, but since the camelry improvised with baggage camels are also mentioned by Herodotos, Babylonian hereditary chariot lands still existed during the reign of Cyrus and scythed chariots later became a regular part of the army, all three gimmicks are included on the off-chance that they were used. The minima apply only if any troops so marked are used other than the camels.

Herodotos mentions a divine standard in a sacred chariot. This would be kept in the camp during battle and so must appear only as one of the baggage elements, and then only if the C-in-C is the Great King in his chariot and Immortals are also used.

61. EARLY CARTHAGINIAN 550 BC - 275 BC

Warm. Ag 3. S, Rv, GH, Wd, O, RF, D, Rd, BUAf, F.
E: 1/7, 1/52, 1/56, 2/5, 2/9, 2/15, 2/27.

C-in-C - Reg Kn (O) @ 31AP if in chariot, Reg Cv (O) @ 28AP if on horse	1
Sub-general - as above	1-2
Regrade C-in-C or sub-general to Reg Sp (S) @ 27AP if commanding Sacred Band	0-1
Carthaginian 4-horse chariots - Reg Kn (O) @ 11AP	0-8
Poeni cavalry - Reg Cv (I) @ 6AP	1-2
Sacred Band - Reg Sp (S) @ 7AP	0-8
Other Poeni citizen infantry - Reg Sp (I) @ 4AP or Reg Ax (O) @ 4AP	0-8
African spearmen - Reg Sp (I) @ 4AP	12-24
Spanish foot with large round shields - Irr Ax (S) @ 4AP	0-8
Spanish skirmishers - Irr Ps (I) @ 1AP or caetrati - Irr Ps (S) @ 3AP	0-1 per 2 Spanish Ax
Balearic slingers - Irr Ps (O) @ 2AP or Reg Ps (O) @ 2AP	0-6
Libyan or Moorish mercenary javelinmen - Irr Ps (I) @ 1AP	8-18
Ligurians - Irr Ax (S) @ 4AP	0, or 4-8
Sardinian, Corsican or Sicel javelinmen - Irr Ax (O) @ 3AP	0, or 4-24
Slingers or Sardinian archers - Irr Ps (O) @ 2AP	0-2
Camp - Irr Bge (O) @ 2AP, or ox-wagons - Irr Bge (I) @ 1AP	0-2 per general
Palisade protecting camp - TF @ 1AP	0, or 1-2 per Bge (O)
Rabble of camp followers - Irr Hd (O) @ 1AP	0, or 1 per Bge
Triremes - Reg Gal (F) @ 4AP [Poeni Ax]	0-6
Transports - Irr Shp (I) @ 2AP [Cv, Kn, Bge]	0-6
Upgrade transports packed with soldiers to supplement galleys to Irr Shp (O) @ 3AP [any foot]	Any

Only in Sicily:

Siciliot allies - List: Early Hoplite Greek (Bk 1/52) or Later Hoplite Greek (Bk 2/5)	
Sicel allies - List: Italian Hill Tribes (Bk 1/36)	

Only if in Africa and before 500 BC:

Makai allies - List: Early Libyan (Bk 1/7)	

Only after 411 BC:

Campanian, Etruscan or Greek cavalry - Reg Cv (O) @ 8AP	0-3
Campanian infantry - Up to ½ Reg Sp (O) @ 5AP, remainder Reg Ax (O) @ 4AP	0-9
Gallic infantry - Irr Wb (O) @ 3AP	0-8

Only after 390 BC:

Heavy non-torsion bolt-shooters - Reg Art (O) @ 8AP	0-2
Replace triremes with quinquiremes - Reg Gal (O) @ 5AP [Poeni Ax]	½ -all

Only after 341 BC:

Numidian light horse - Irr LH (O) @ 4AP	0-6
Greek mercenary hoplites - Reg Sp (O) @ 5AP	0-8

Only if in Africa from 309 BC:

Numidian allies - List: Numidian or Early Moorish (Bk 2/40)	

The city of Carthage started as a colony planted by a Phoenician rebel queen on the North African coast in modern Tunisia. It grew into a powerful trading state that was to become Rome's most dangerous rival. It quickly began to flex military muscles and planted colonies of its own, notably in the western part of Sicily where it came into confrontation with first Syracuse and then Rome. This list covers Carthaginian armies from Mago's institution of a largely mercenary army until the end of the war against Pyrrhos of Epeiros. The tactics of early Carthaginian armies were uninspired. Without Hannibal's genius to make optimum use of the different capabilities of their varied mercenary troops, the heterogeneity of their forces was a liability rather than an asset. 4th century Carthaginian armies relied mainly on the phalanx of close order spearmen. After their defeat at Krimisos in 341 BC, the Carthaginians began to hire Greek mercenaries because they thought them "the best and most warlike troops available anywhere", which implies that their own Libyan spearmen, probably reluctant conscripts at this period, were not as good. The recent identification of a statue with bronze attachment points for a quiver/bowcase and spear as representing the Carthaginian general Hamilcar suggests that Carthaginian chariots were based on eastern rather than Libyan models, hence the new classification as Kn. Their superiority over Sicilian Greek cavalry at Krimisos and their (albeit unsuccessful) frontal charge against hoplites at Tunis also suggests aggressive use, confirming the appropriateness of the classification. Early Carthaginian cavalry were markedly inferior to Siciliot Greeks. Campanian cavalry allowed to dismount do so as Sp (O), their shields having been brought up by servants. The Libyan Makai helped Carthage destroy an attempted African colony led by the Spartan Dorieus about 513. There is no evidence in this era of high quality African Ps. Numidian allies Ps (S) must be downgraded to (I) @ 1AP. Before the scutum was introduced at the end of the 3rd century BC, most Spanish foot used large round shields. Whether there were skirmishers from the start and how soon these adopted the small round caetra shield is uncertain. Hopefully, wargames generals will be able to supply the necessary genius to lift this army out of its tactical rut, and thus avoid execution for their failure, the standard Carthaginian method of encouragement. Only one ally contingent can be used.

62. LYKIAN 546 BC - 300 BC

Warm. Ag 1. S, Rv, **DH**, CH, WH, CH, SH, Wd, V, RF, Rd, BUAf, F.
E: 1/52, 1/60, 2/5, 2/12, 2/16, 2/19.

C-in-C - Irr Cv (O) @ 17AP	1
Sub-general - as above	0-1
Ally-general - Irr Cv (O) @ 12AP	0-2
Cavalry - Irr Cv (O) @ 7AP	5-9
Warriors - Irr Ax (O) @ 3AP	32-96
Upgrade warriors to Lykian hoplites - Irr Sp (O) @ 4AP	16-60
Hillmen with drepanon - Irr Bd (F) @ 5AP	0-12
Archers - Irr Ps (O) @ 2AP	6-12
Peasants - Irr Ps (I) @ 1AP	0-12
Camp - Irr Bge (O) @ 2AP, or pack-donkeys or ox-wagons - Irr Bge (I) @ 1AP	0-2 per general
Pentekonters or pirate hemiolae - Reg Gal (I) @ 3AP [Bw (O)], or lembi - Irr Bts (O) @ 2AP [Ax (I)]	0-3
Marines - Irr Bw (O) @ 4AP	1 per Gal
Pirates - Irr Ax (I) @ 2AP	1 per Bts

Only before 500 BC:	
Replace cavalry by chariots - Irr Cv (O) @ 16AP if C-in-C or sub-general, 11AP if ally-general, otherwise 6AP	0-4

Only after 526 BC:	
Trieres - Reg Gal (F) @ 4AP [Bw (O)]	0-2

Only from 425 BC:	
Mercenary hoplites - Reg Sp (O) @ 5AP	0-8
Mercenary peltasts - Reg Ps (S) @ 3AP	0-2
Mercenary archers and slingers - Reg Ps (O) @ 2AP	0-2

Only from 323 BC:	
Replace Reg Ps (S) with Reg Ax (O) @ 4AP.	All

This list covers the armies of the Lykian princes from Cyrus's conquest of western Asia Minor until the annexation of Lykia by Pleistarchos after Ipsos. From then on, Lykia was nominally subject to a succession of major states culminating with Rome, though this did not prevent them squabbling with neighbours, aiding factions or indulging in piracy, which minor conflicts are not covered due to lack of information. Lightly-armed Lykian soldiers of the period covered are frequently depicted fighting alongside hoplites who may be Greek mercenaries or native Lykians. Although nominally vassals of Persia, the Lykian princes were to all practical purposes independent, although they would often co-operate with Achaemenid satraps. The Karaburun tumulus shows an unarmoured Lykian foot soldier with javelin and hoplon. The Trysa heroon (circa 385 BC) shows Lykian infantry with helmets, hoplon shields and the drepanon, a vicious scythe-like sword used one-handed. Herodotos says that the drepanon was a traditional Lykian weapon. However, a recent paper suggests that the drepanon wielders depicted in art are in fact Milyan hillmen. Tombs from Lykia "proper" show an overwhelming majority of hoplites from as early as the 6th century, but are likely to have been erected by the more prosperous inhabitants. Prettier than the usual rag-bag hillmen, with tunics in a variety of bright colours and tasteful accessories!

63. PAIONIAN 512 BC - 284 BC

Cool. Ag 3. Rv, DH, SH, Wd, BF, Rd, BUA, F.
E: 1/47, 1/48, 1/54, 1/60, 2/12, 2/17, 2/18, 2/30.

C-in-C - Irr LH (O) @ 14AP or Irr Ax (S) @ 14AP	1
Sub-general - Irr LH (O) @ 15AP or Irr Ps (S) @ 13AP or Irr Ax (O) @ 13AP	1-2
Cavalry - Irr LH (O) @ 4AP	6-12
Hypaspists - Irr Ax (S) @ 4AP	0-5
Warriors - Irr Ps (S) @ 3AP or Irr Ax (O) @ 3AP	40-129
Slingers or archers - Irr Ps (O) @ 2AP	4-12
Levies - Irr Ps (I) @ 1AP or Irr Ax (I) @ 2AP	16-33
War dogs - Irr Wb (F) @ 2AP	0-1
Lembi - Irr Bts (O) @ 2AP [Ps (S) or Ax (O)]	0-4
Camp - Irr Bge (O) @ 2AP, or ox-wagons - Irr Bge (I) @ 1AP, or pack-ponies - Irr Bge (F) @ 2AP	0-2 per general
Illyrian allies - List: Illyrian (Bk 1/47)	

Only in 310 BC:

Macedonian allies - List: Macedonian Early Successor (Bk 2/18)	

This list covers the armies of the Paionian tribes, including the Eastern Paionians, the Agrianians and the Kingdom of Paionia from their first contact with the Persians until the annexation of the Kingdom of Paionia by Lysimachos. A combined army of Paionians and Illyrians fought Parmenion's Macedonians in 356 BC. Kassandros brought Macedonian troops to the aid of King Audoleon against the Illyrians in 310 BC. Macedonians cannot be used with Illyrians.

64. EARLY JAPANESE 500 BC - 500 AD:

Cool. Ag 1 before 275 AD, then 2. S, Rv, **DH**, SH, Wd, O, E, SF or BF. BUAf if Yayoi. Rd if Kofun.
E: 1/64, 2/75, 2/76, 2/77.

Camp - Irr Bge (O) @ 2AP, or porters - Irr Bge (I) @ 1AP	0-2 per general
Boats - Irr Bts (O) @ 2AP [any foot]	0-6

Only Yayoi culture from 500 BC to 274 AD:

C-in-C - Irr Bw (I) @ 13AP, or Irr Bd (I) @ 14 AP, or Irr Ax (S) @ 14AP	1
Ally-general of same nation - Irr Bw (I) @ 8AP, or Irr Bd (I) @ 9AP, or Irr Ax (S) @ 9AP	1-3
Upgrade ally-general to sub-general - Irr Bw (I) @ 13AP, or Irr Bd (I) @ 14 AP, or Irr Ax (S) @ 14AP	0-1
Upgrade Bge element of C-in-C's command to priestess-queen in litter or man-draft cart - Irr Bge (S) @ 3AP	0 or 1
Dagger-axe men - Irr Bd (I) @ 4AP	12-30
Spearmen - Irr Ax (S) @ 4AP	12-30
Archers - Irr Bw (I) @ 3AP	40-84
Regrade foot with big shields, spearmen as Irr Pk (X) @ 3AP or archers as Irr Bw (O) @ 4AP	0-12
Upgrade archers to crossbowmen - Irr Bw (O) @ 4AP	0-2
Replace archers with slingers - Irr Ps (O) @ 2AP	Any

Only Kofun culture from 275 AD:

C-in-C as uji archers - Irr Bw (S) @ 15AP	1
Sub-general - Irr Bw (S) @ 15AP	0-2
Ally-general - Irr Bw (S) @ 10AP	0-2
Uji nobles and toneri retainers as armoured archers with pavise - Irr Bw (S) @ 5AP	12-30
Other retainers with less armour - Irr Bw (O) @ 4AP	1-2 per Bw (S)
Uji nobles, toneri and yatsuko retainers as spearmen - Irr Pk (X) @ 3AP	1-2 per 3 Bw (S) or (O)
Be (levy archers) - Irr Bw (I) @ 3AP	0-16

Only Kofun culture from 360 AD:

Transports - Irr Shp (I) @ 2AP [any]	0-6
Paekche or Kaya allies - List: Paekche and Kaya Korean (Bk 2/75)	

Only Kofun culture from 408 AD:

Upgrade generals to Irr Cv (O) @ 17AP if C-in-C or sub-general, 12AP if ally-general	Any
Further upgrade Cv (O) generals with armoured horses to Irr Kn (I) @ 18AP if C-in-C or 13AP if ally-general	0-1
Armoured horse archers - Irr Cv (O) @ 7AP	0-2
Pacified Emishi archers - Irr Ps (O) @ 2AP	0-2

This list covers Japanese armies of the Yayoi and early Kofun cultures. Its first part represents the Yayoi culture. Continental immigrants mixing with the local people of the neolithic Jomon culture established a rice-farming, iron- and bronze-using culture that soon covered the entire Japanese archipelago except Hokkaido and the Ryukyu islands. The Yayoi were not united and even their most powerful rulers controlled only alliances of semi-independent communities, hence the limited sub-general allowed. Chinese sources say that over 100 "Wa" (Japanese) states existed. They were centred on fortified settlements whose moats, palisades and towers indicate frequent internecine warfare. The most important was Yamatai, in either north Kyushu or western Honshu, ruled approx AD 183-248 by the priestess-queen Himiko. She lived in seclusion in a palisaded palace surrounded by armed guards, "occupying herself with magic and sorcery" and attended only by women, while her brother was the public face of the régime. Over 20 statelets were reckoned as her subjects. Despite Himiko's seclusion we allow such a priestess-queen to be fielded for local colour, in the hope that her total isolation may have been exaggerated by Chinese sources or that other such female rulers (such as her successor Iyo, c.250 to sometime after 266) may not have followed her practice so strictly. Warriors wore simple clothing and tattoos, and fought with spears, dagger-axes, swords, wooden bows with the lower limb shorter than the upper, and slings. We assume archers were in the majority, as in later periods, though some regions favoured the sling over the bow. Spears were 2-3 metres long. Shields were mostly light and of moderate size. One surviving very large shield could have been used to protect an archer or a spearman. Some wooden armour has been found. At first both bronze and iron weapons were used, iron becoming predominant before the end of the period.

The Kofun period saw great increases in the use of iron armour (of laced plates in Chinese style and cuirasses of vertical strips in Korean style from which the tankoh plate cuirass was developed), the gradual consolidation of most of Japan under an Imperial dynasty based in the Yamato basin and claiming descent from the Sun goddess, military interventions in Korea and the first small introduction of cavalry. Armies of 10-25,000 men were common. The members and retainers of the aristocratic clans called uji provided the backbone of the army, mostly fighting as archers with iron armour and large leather shields, treated here as portable pavises justifying grading as Bw (S). Others were armed with spears, at least some of which were 4 metres long. Combined with pavises, this suggests they should be Pk (X). The lower classes were either directly dependent on the uji or organised into guilds called be; the be certainly supplied troops, and others may have done as well. The introduction of cavalry, and the lamellar keikoh armour they wore, was probably inspired by defeats of Japanese infantry against Koguryo cavalry around 400 AD. In 408 AD a large-scale immigration from the former Chinese commanderies in Korea may have contributed to the introduction of mounted archery; cavalry are mentioned occasionally in the 5th century (when there is even some evidence for Korean-style horse-armour) and were to become more common in the 6th. Although major conquests of Emishi territory had yet to start, a few Emishi were already recruited by 479 AD.

ALPHABETICAL INDEX OF BOOK 1 ARMY LISTS

ALPHABETICAL INDEX OF BOOK 1 ARMY LISTS

ALPHABETICAL INDEX OF BOOK 1 ARMY LISTS

GEOGRAPHIC INDEX TO ALL DBMM ARMY LISTS

AFRICA

Egypt.
1/2 Early Egyptian 3000BC-1541BC.
1/17 Hyksos 1645BC-1537BC.
1/22 New-Kingdom Egyptian 1543BC- 1069BC.
1/38 Libyan Egyptian 946BC-712BC.
1/46 Kushite Egyptian 745BC-593BC.
1/53 Saitic Egyptian 664BC-335BC.
1/58 Meroitic Kushite 592BC-350AD.
2/20 Ptolemaic Egyptian 320BC-30BC.
3/49 Tulunid Egyptian. 868AD-905AD.
3/49 Iqshidid Egyptian. 935AD-969AD.
3/66 Fatimid Egyptian. 969AD-1171AD.
4/20 Ayyubid Egyptian 1171AD-1250AD.
4/45 Mamluk Egyptian 1250AD-1517AD.

Other Africa.
1/3 Nubian 3000BC-1480BC.
1/7 Early Libyan 3000BC-70AD.
1/61 Early Carthaginian 550BC-275BC
2/32 Later Carthaginian. 275BC-146BC.
2/40 Numidian or Early Moorish. 215BC-25AD.
2/55 Nobades, Blemmye or Beja. 30BC-1500 AD.
2/57 Later Moorish. 25AD-696AD.
2/62 Abyssinian & Horn of Africa. 100AD-1529AD .
2/84 African Vandal. 442AD-535AD.
3/12 Christian Nubian. 550AD-1500AD.
3/33 Early Muslim North Africa 696AD-1160AD.
3/69 West Sudanese. 1000AD-1591AD.
3/70 Tuareg. 1000AD-1880AD.
3/75 Islamic Berber. 1039AD-1529AD.

AMERICA (& the Pacific)

North America.
4/ 9 Eastern Forest American. c1100AD-1620AD.
4/10 Mound Builder American. c1100AD-1701AD.
4/11 North-Western American. c1100AD-1770AD.

South America.
3/22 Maya 600AD-1546AD.
3/41 Chichimec & Pueblo Cultures 800AD-1500AD.
3/59 Toltec. 930AD-1168AD.
4/12 Hawaiian c1100AD-1785AD.
4/19 Tarascan or Toltec-Chichimec 1168AD-1521AD.
4/29 Tupi. 1200AD-1601AD.
4/53 Mixtec or Zapotec. 1280AD-1523AD.
4/63 Aztec. 1325AD-1521AD.
4/70 Chanca. 1350AD-1440AD.
4/71 Chimu. 1350AD-1464AD.
4/72 Amazonian. 1350AD-1662AD.
4/81 Inca. 1438AD-1534AD.
4/84 Mapuce 1461AD-1552AD

Pacific.
4/12 Polynesian or Melanesian. 1100AD-1785AD.

ASIA

Arabia
1/6 Early Bedouin 3000 BC-312BC.
1/8 Makkan, Dilmun, Saba Ma'in & Qataban 2800BC-312BC
2/23 Later pre-Islamic Arab 312BC-633AD.
3/25 Arab Conquest. 622AD-660AD.

ASIA

Arabia
3/25 Khawarij 658AD–873AD.
3/31 Umayyad Arab. 661AD-750AD.
3/37 Abbasid Arab. 747AD-945AD.
3/50 Zanj Revolt 869AD – 883AD.
3/54 Dynastic Bedouin. 890AD-1150AD.
3/54 Qaramita 897AD-1078AD.
4/46 Ilkhanid. 1251AD-1355AD

Black Sea
1/16 Hittite Old & Middle Kingdom 1680BC-1380BC..
1/24 Hittite Empire 1380 BC - 1180 BC.
1/31 Neo-Hittite & Later Aramaean. 1100BC - 710 BC.
1/39 Urartian 880BC-585BC.
1/40 Phrygian 850BC-676BC.
1/43 Skythian & Massagetae 750BC-70AD.
1/50 Lydian 687BC-540BC.
2/6 Bithynian 435BC-74BC.
2/25 Bosporan 310 BC-107 BC & 10 BC - 375 AD.
2/48 Mithridatic. 110BC-47BC.
2/65 Tervingi or Early Visigothic. 200AD-419AD.
2/67 Greuthingi & Early Ostrogothic 200AD-493AD.
2/67 Herul, Sciri & Taifali. 200AD-493AD.
3/14 Early Bulgar 674AD-1018AD.
3/47 Pecheneg. 850AD-1122AD.
3/51 Bagratid Armenian 885AD-1045AD
3/71 Georgian 1008AD-1683AD
3/80 Cuman (Kipchak). 1054AD-1394AD.
4/47 Successors of the Golden Horde 1502AD-1556AD.
4/49 Anatolian Turkoman 1260AD-1515AD

Byzantium.
3/4 Early Byzantine 493AD-578AD.
3/17 Maurikian Byzantine. 575AD-650AD
3/26 Early Serbian & Croatian 627AD-1189AD.
3/29 Thematic Byzantine. 650AD-963AD.
3/76 Konstantinian Byzantine. 1042AD-1073 AD.
3/65 Nikephorian Byzantine. 963AD-1042AD.
4/1 Komnenan Byzantine 1071AD-1204AD.
4/2 Cilician Armenian 1071AD-1375AD.
4/31 Nikaian Byzantine. 1204AD-1261AD
4/32 Romanian Frank. 1204AD-1311AD.
4/33 Epirot Byzantine. 1204AD-1340AD.
4/34 Trapezuntine Byzantine. 1204AD-1461AD.
4/50 Palaiologan Byzantine. 1261AD-1384AD.
4/51 Morean Byzantine. 1262AD-1460AD.
4/55 Ottoman. 1281AD-1512AD.

Mesopotamia, Syria & Near East
1/1 Sumerian 3000BC-2334BC & 2250BC.
1/4 Zagros & Anatolian Highland 3000BC-950BC.
1/9 Early Syrian 2700BC-2200BC.
1/11 Akkad 2334BC-2193BC & Ur 2112BC-2004BC.
1/12 Sumerian Successor States 2028 BC-1460BC.
1/15 Later Amorite 1894BC-1595BC.
1/19 Mitanni 1595BC-1274BC.
1/20 Syro-Canaanite or Ugaritic 1592BC-1100 BC.
1/21 Kassite & later Babylonian 1595BC-747BC.
1/25 Assyrian & Early Neo-Assyrian 1365BC-745BC.
1/27 Early Hebrew c1250 BC - 1000 BC.
1/29 Philistine 1166BC-600BC.

GEOGRAPHIC INDEX TO ALL DBMM ARMY LISTS

EUROPE

Greece & Balkans
1/18 Minoan & Early Mycenaean 1600BC-1250BC.
1/26 Later Mycenean & Trojan War 1250BC-1190 BC.
1/28 Sea People 1208BC-1176BC.
1/30 Dark-Age & Geometric Greece. 1160BC- 650BC.
1/47 Illyrian 700BC-10AD.
1/48 Thracian 700BC-46AD
1/52 Early Hoplite Greece 669 BC-449BC.
1/54 Early Macedonian 650BC-355BC.
1/56 Kyrenean Greek 630BC-74BC.
1/63 Paionian 512BC-284BC.
2/5 Later Hoplite Greek 448BC-225BC.
2/12 Alexandrian Macedonian 359BC-319BC.
2/15 Alexandrian Imperial. 328BC-321BC.
2/17 Lysimachid. 320BC-281BC.
2/18 Macedonian Early Successor 320BC-260BC.
2/31 Hellenistic Greek 278BC-146BC.
2/34 Attalid Pergamene. 263BC-129BC.
2/35 Later Macedonian. 260BC-148BC.
2/52 Dacian. 60BC-106AD & Carpi 106AD-380AD.
4/22 Serbian Empire 1180AD-1459AD
4/25 Later Bulgar 1186AD-1395AD
4/56 Order of St John 1291AD-1522AD
4/60 Catalan Compnay 1302AD-1388AD
4/69 Albanian. 1345-1430AD & 1443AD-1479AD.

Italy & the Alps
1/14 European Bronze & Iron Age 2000 BC-315BC.
1/33 Villanovan Italian 1000BC-650BC
1/36 Italian Hill Tribes 1000BC-124BC.
1/55 Latin & Early-Roman, 650BC-290BC.
1/55 Early Etruscan & Umbrian 650BC-290BC.
1/57 Etruscan League 600BC-280BC.
1/59 Tullian Roman 578BC-400BC.
2/8 Campanian & Apulian 420BC-203BC.
2/8 Lucanian & Bruttian 420BC-203BC.
2/9 Syracusan 410BC-210BC
2/10 Camillan Roman. 400BC-275BC.
2/13 Samnite. 355BC-272BC.
2/27 Pyrrhic 300 BC-272BC.
2/33 Polybian Roman. 275BC-105BC.
2/45 Sicilian & Italian Slave Revolts. 135BC-71BC.
2/49 Marian Roman. 105BC-25BC.
2/56 Early Imperial Roman. 25BC-197AD.
2/64 Middle Imperial Roman. 193AD-324AD.
2/78 Late Imperial Roman. 307AD-408 AD.
3/3 Italian Ostrogothic. 493AD-561AD.
2/82 Patrician Roman 408 AD – 493 AD
3/21 Italian Lombard. 584AD-1076AD.
3/73 Communal Italian. 1029AD-1320AD.
3/33 Early Muslim Sicily. 696AD-1160AD.
3/77 Papal Italian. 1049AD-1320AD.
4/5 Sicilian. 1072AD-1442AD.
4/61 Italian Condotta. 1320AD-1495AD.
4/41 Early Swiss. 1240AD-1400AD.
4/79 Later Swiss. 1400AD-1522AD

Scandinavia & Baltic
2/73 Old Saxon etc. 250AD-804AD.
3/40 Norse Viking and Leidang. 790AD-1280AD.

EUROPE
4/18 Lithuanian or Samogitian. 1132AD-1435AD
4/27 Estonian. 1200AD-1227AD.
4/28 Prussian. 1200AD-1283AD.
4/54 Medieval Scandinavian. 1280AD-1523AD.

Spain & Portugal
2/39 Ancient Spanish. 240BC-20BC.
2/66 Early Vandal. 200AD-442AD.
2/83 Later Visigothic 419 AD – 720 AD.
3/34 Andalusian. 710AD-1172AD.
3/35 Feudal Spanish. 718AD-1340AD
4/38 Murcian & Granadine. 1232AD-1492AD.
4/60 Catalan Company. 1302AD-1388AD
4/68 Medieval Spanish & Portuguese 1340AD-1485A
4/74 Free Company or Armagnac. 1357AD-1444AD.

INDIA
1/10 Melukhkhan Indian 2700BC-1500 BC.
1/10 pre-Vedic Indian 2700BC-1500 BC.
1/23 Vedic Indian 1500BC-512BC.
2/1 Republican Indian 500BC-321BC
2/2 Mountain Indian 500BC-170BC
2/3 Classical Indian 500BC-545AD.
2/36 Graeco-Bactrian 250BC-130BC.
2/36 Graeco-Indian 170BC-55BC.
2/42 Tamil Indian and Sinhalese. 175BC-1515AD
2/46 Kushan. 135BC-477AD.
3/10 Hindu Indian. 545AD-1510AD.
3/38 Arab Indian 751AD-1206AD
3/64 Ghaznavid. 962AD-1186AD.
4/ 8 Ghurid. 1100AD-1215AD.
4/36 Later Muslim Indian. 1206AD-1526AD.

ORIENT

China.
1/13 Hsia & Shang Chinese 2000BC-1017BC.
1/14 Chinese Border Tribes 2000BC-315BC.
1/32 Western Chou Chinese 1100BC- 480BC.
1/32 Early "Spring & Autumn" 1100BC-480BC
1/43 Early Hu Chinese 300BC-70AD.
2/4 Warring States Chinese 480BC-202BC.
2/4 Yueh Chinese 480 BC - 333 BC.
2/4 Ch'u Chinese 480BC-202BC.
2/4 Ch'in Chinese 350BC-221BC.
2/4 Chao Chinese 307BC-202BC.
2/21 Ch'iang & Ti Chinese 315BC-550AD.
2/29 Tien & K'un-Ming Chinese 295BC-45AD
2/38 Hsiung-nu & Juan-juan. 250BC-555AD.
2/41 Han Chinese. 202BC-189AD.
2/61 Hsien-pi, Wu-huan, Khitan & Hsi. 90-1000AD.
2/63 Three Kingdoms Chinese. 189AD-316AD
2/63 Western Ts'in (Chin) Chinese. 189AD-316AD.
2/79 Northern & Southern Dynasties. 317AD-589AD.
3/20 Sui & Early T'ang Chinese. 581AD-755AD
3/23 Khmer & Cham. 605AD-1471 AD.
3/36 Nan-chao. 728AD-1253AD.
3/39 Late T'ang & 5 Dynasties Chinese. 755AD-979AD.
3/56 Khitan-Liao. 907AD-1125AD.
3/56 Khitan-Liao. 907AD-1125AD.
3/62 Sung Chinese. 960AD-1279AD.

GEOGRAPHIC INDEX TO ALL DBMM ARMY LISTS

ORIENT

China
3/67 Hsi-Hsia. 982AD-1227AD
4/14 Jurchen-Chin. 1114AD-1234AD.
4/15 Qara-Khitan. 1124AD-1211AD.
4/48 Yuan Chinese. 1260AD-1368AD.
4/73 Ming Chinese. 1356AD-1598AD

Korea.
2/75 Paekche & Kaya Korean. 300AD-663 AD.
2/76 Koguryo Korean. 300AD-668AD.
2/77 Shilla Korean. 300AD-935AD.
4/78 Yi Dynasty Korean. 1392AD-1598AD.
3/57 Koryo Dynasty Korean. 918AD-1392AD.

Indonesia & Malaya.
4/37 Indonesian & Malayan. 1222AD-1511AD.

ORIENT

Japan
1/64 Early Japanese 500BC-500AD.
3/6 Emishi. 500AD-878AD.
3/7 Pre-Samurai Japanese. 500AD-900AD
3/55 Early Samurai. 900AD-1300AD.
4/59 Post-Mongol Samurai. 1300AD-1542AD

South-East Asia
1/49 Early Vietnamese 700 BC - 938 AD.
3/9 Burmese. 500AD-1526AD.
3/60 Medieval Vietnamese. 939AD-1527AD
4/37 Indonesian & Malayan 1222AD-1511AD.
4/40 Siamese. 1238AD-1518AD

Tibet..
3/15 Tibetan. 560AD-1065AD

ALPHABETICAL INDEX TO ALL DBMM ARMY LISTS

ALPHABETICAL INDEX TO ARMY LISTS

ALPHABETICAL INDEX TO ALL DBMM ARMY LISTS

ALPHABETICAL INDEX TO ALL DBMM ARMY LISTS

ALPHABETICAL INDEX TO ALL DBMM ARMY LISTS

Made in United States
Orlando, FL
15 July 2024

49010530R00054